STARS AND WARS

STARS AND WARS

THE FILM MEMOIRS AND PHOTOGRAPHS OF
ALAN TOMKINS

WITH GARETH OWEN

FOREWORD BY
OLIVER STONE

The History Press

First published 2015

The History Press
The Mill, Brimscombe Port
Stroud, Gloucestershire, GL5 2QG
www.thehistorypress.co.uk

British Library Cataloguing in Publication
Data.
A catalogue record for this book is
available from the British Library.

ISBN 978 0 7509 5617 8

Design by Katie Beard
Printed in Great Britain

Contents

Foreword by Oliver Stone

Alan Tomkins looks the part – post-Second World War British film, fair-skinned, eagle-eyed and always willing to give it his best, to whom life is a toy train set under a Christmas tree. Young Alan would've delighted himself for hours in unboxing the gift and erecting a gigantic labyrinth across the basement floor. The figurines of conductors and passengers would be the actors, and no doubt an adult might troop in to supervise and pat young Alan on his shoulder, 'Wonderful job, my boy!' This would be the director!

Alan, as you may know, became an art director. I gather he never wanted to be a production designer. There's a difference. A production designer has to engage with the director on an almost daily basis and explain himself to budgetarians and producers, etc. An art director is hired by the production designer and works mainly for him. The art director goes from job to job, set to set, film to film, sometimes at the halfway point. Sometimes he replaces somebody who quits, or is fired, or is sick. An art director is a samurai. He is known inside a loop. If his reputation is stained by any mishap, such as an accident, a miscommunication, or even worse, an underestimation of cost, his reputation may well be grievously damaged, and he may not work again inside that self-referencing loop called 'British Film' or 'Hollywood' for a long, long time.

The art director's life has little to do with real life. Indeed, Mr Tomkins barely mentions that he has a wife somewhere in these fifty years of film-making. (The only time Alan departed from his role as a craftsman was, apparently, when he shyly directed Paul Newman in a scene from a John Huston movie, *Mackintosh Man*.) You would not know if he had children, or if he had a normal life of any kind outside his work. But you will learn a great deal about film. You will learn what is crucial. To an art director, it's how to *think* something through and through, to design and then build, with budget, a set or location that *truly* works for a film, which is far harder than you think. Great sets exist, but do they serve the film? The sets Alan plays with have grown from toys into such material as whales, tanks, planes, fireworks, ships, gardens, rooms, houses, shops, and fantasies of all kinds.

Reading Alan's memoirs makes us see the movie world as only a craftsman might see it. As a result, we have here a torrent of great movies rumbling by (*Lawrence of Arabia*, *Dr No*, *2001: A Space Odyssey*, *The Empire Strikes Back*, *Victor Victoria*, *Saving Private Ryan*, *Batman Begins*, *Casino Royale*). A modest and highly practical Tomkins doesn't take much note about the multitude of stars he's worked with (Sean Connery, Peter O'Toole, Richard Attenborough, Laurence Olivier, Julie Andrews, Kevin Costner, and Tom Hanks), they are passengers on his sets, ghosts in a landscape.

What he does take true joy in is meeting his real-life heroes – mostly Second World War vets, such as Lord Dowding, Group Captain Douglas Bader, Wing Commander Bob Stanford Tuck and Squadron Leader Ginger Lacey, from a time which clearly marked the boy in the London Blitz of 1940–41. (Thus, *The Heroes of Telemark*, *Battle of Britain*, *Hanover Street*, *A Bridge too Far* and *Memphis Belle* – five British-made Second World War spectacles.)

Mr Tomkins, at a later point in his career, crossed my path on three films in a row, working for production designer Victor Kempster (*JFK*, *Heaven & Earth* and *Natural Born Killers*). I was very proud to have

Mr Tomkins with us, as he represented the tradition of British film-making that Hollywood admires. He made my films better.

But then again, I wish he'd been less the British min-imalist (think Anthony Hopkins in *Remains of the Day*) in describing his journey. We all know films are made with blood, sweat, and tears (some in fact real.) All the sweet speeches following a successful outcome are opiates to relieve that hurt. But then again, Alan lacks a malicious bone. Whenever he expresses any such feeling, it is generally through omission. Several actors and directors are thus not given names. I'm happy to see my own name has stayed in the mix.

It was an honour to work with Alan, and I hope that during the course of their working lives, a director has such an experience with a true 'English art director'.

Thank you, Alan, for these memoirs. They ennoble your craft.

Oliver Stone
Los Angeles

▲ Oliver Stone offering Kevin Costner a few thoughts on the courtroom scene.

Preface

A couple of years ago I was encouraged by friends to write some of my adventures in the film business down in book form; it was actually something my wife was all for, too, as she said it was about time I didn't bore just her with all my stories.

But how do you condense a life and career across scores of films into an interesting volume, when so much of my work as a draughtsman, assistant and then art director has been relatively technical? Well, I think you do it by perhaps choosing a couple of dozen of the best, most enjoyable, most fulfilling and perhaps most successful films you've worked on – at least I hope so, because that's exactly what I've done here.

I won't bore you with long synopses or plot lines, nor the technicalities of the drawing board, but what I will do is tell you about the wonderful locations, terrific stars and interesting problems I've encountered in my fifty year career. I've been incredibly lucky, and I hope you enjoy sharing a little of my luck now.

– AT

1 Starting Out

People often ask how I began my long career in the film industry. Looking back, it seems the answer lies in my making all the wrong decisions ... but they turned out to be decisions that set me off in a much better direction than I'd ever dreamed possible.

Having finished my schooling, and armed with some good exam results, I (wrongly) decided to enjoy one last long summer holiday before starting work and, perhaps, thereafter only having a couple of weeks each year. It was a month and a half later before I started chasing up some local apprenticeships for draughtsmen and model-makers and, of course, by then my eager school chums had snapped up all the decent ones!

In desperation I visited the youth employment office in Barnet, and took along some of my drawings, thinking they would sell me nicely as a draughtsman. I was duly offered a position as trainee chef on a luxury liner, which served only to conjure up visions of me peeling potatoes as I looked out of a porthole in some very hot harbour in the Middle East. As I couldn't even grill a piece of toast successfully, I thanked him and declined. Scratching his head, the careers advisor thought about giving his cousin – the personnel manager at Elstree Studios – a call. As (my) luck would have it, they'd just fired their young art department apprentice for being in trouble with the police once

◄ ABPC Studios, Elstree, where I started my working life.

too often, and asked me 'How would you like to start Monday?'

Up until that time, my only experience of a film studio was when I used to cycle past Riverside Studios in Hammersmith and, occasionally, I'd wait near the big doors on the street for them to open. Once, in 1949, I remember seeing a model street laid out on the stage (quite possibly for *Daughter of Darkness*) and thinking how exciting it all was.

On my first day at Elstree's ABPC (Associated British Picture Company) Studios I knew all eyes would be on me, and I'd have to behave impeccably and, indeed, prove my worth after the way my predecessor had parted company with them.

My first job was as a print boy, taking construction drawings, printing them and then distributing them all around the various departments. I was then given a drawing board and asked to trace a plan of a set. I felt terribly proud of my precisely copied plan, with all the detailed dimensions added in, but the resident designer, Terence Verity, simply whipped it off my desk, tore it in half and placed it over an outline of a film stage – for positioning ideas – and then pretty much discarded it. I learnt a valuable lesson – always ask for more details about the task before you invest too much time and effort into it!

I was very lucky to have two excellent teachers, Peter Glazier and George Richardson, and each gave their time to show me all the skills needed in producing set plans, drawings of fireplaces, doors, windows etc., and always with an eye on the economies of the budget. Over the next three years I progressed from simple details to drawing up my first entire set – a prostitute's flat in Rome, for the film *Interpol*, starring Victor Mature and Anita Ekberg; though my first actual set sketch was for a mountain hut, set against a rock face, for *Don't Bother to Knock*, starring Richard

Todd and Elke Sommer – well, I do like to name-drop occasionally.

I was also given great encouragement from another notable art director, Carmen Dillon, who won an Oscar for Olivier's *Hamlet* in 1948. In fact, I soon realised one big advantage of being an employee at a parent studio was that they sold my services to visiting designers, and with it my base for future work possibilities grew. For instance, I worked with Ken Adam (now 'Sir Ken') on what was his first film as production designer – *Night of the Demon* in 1957, starring Dana Andrews and Peggy Cummins. When Ken returned to make another film at the studio, he specifically asked for me – and that's how I came to work on *The Trials of Oscar Wilde* (1960) and indeed, subsequently, the first James Bond film, *Dr No* in 1962.

Another top designer, Don Ashton, next arrived at Elstree, having recently completed working for David Lean on *Bridge on the River Kwai*, to film *Indiscreet* with Cary Grant and Ingrid Bergman. I have to admit the sets were something very special. It was the first time I had seen slightly curved six-panelled doors fit into a circular wall – carpentry skills at their highest. All the carpets were real too, and not just coloured hessian as was the norm. Happily, I went on to form a good friendship with Don, but he left the industry to concentrate on grand hotel designs which proved quite fortuitous for me, as in-between films I could almost always rely on him to give me some draughting work for bars, restaurants and bedrooms in Sheratons and Holiday Inns somewhere in the world.

At the same time *Indiscreet* was filming in 1958, Sophia Loren and William Holden were shooting Second World War adventure *The Key* on another stage, and when word came through that they were wrapping at 4.30 p.m., as the thick London smog descended, the studio soon emptied. As I lived locally I wasn't in so much of a rush as the others, and we eventually made our way out of the complex. My young assistant, Robin, and I took a look at the particular set they'd been using that day – it was a bedroom scene. Robin, quick as a flash, jumped onto the bed and said 'It's still warm!' That's the closest he, or I, ever got to the lovely warmth of Sophia Loren.

Whilst I was working with Tony Hancock on *The Rebel* in 1961, in which he plays a budding artist and travels to Paris to set up his studio in an attic, someone noticed that the script said he was 'going through his blue period'. For reasons unknown to me, they proposed he have a Jersey cow, painted that very colour, tied up in his room. With the help of one of the unit painters, I made up a bucket of mid-blue emulsion and soap powder (which helps to wash it all off) and, with brush in hand, greeted my four-legged friend in plenty of time for its post-lunchtime *Avatar* cameo. However, just before it was due to be led on stage, word came through that the RSPCA were on their way over to inspect the beast and I was given the order to 'wash it all off, now!'

You really can't make it up ...

On that same film, Tony's character had a scene as a pavement artist outside the Tate Gallery (see photos on pp. 8 and 13) and I was asked to go into London, look at some pavement artists and their work and then, just prior to the Sunday afternoon shoot, chalk some pictures. The weather forecast was for rain, so I decided to have a plan B with some chalked cards I could hang from the railing, in case my other work was washed away. When the electricians arrived to set up, they tossed a flat cap down next to my drawings and I chalked '*Grazie*', '*Danke*' and 'Thank You'. We collected a few bob that morning!

◄ Tony Hancock, the lonely genius.

▼ A blue cow?

▲ Irene Handl played the wonderful landlady. 'It's a self-portrait!' ... 'Who of?'

Luckily the rain didn't materialise, but it did sadden me to think that I, and all the other artists, had to walk away from our best work at the end of the day.

Oh! As my first Christmas at ABPC loomed large I was told it was customary that the young apprentice bought a bottle of gin or scotch for the office party. I felt sure it was a wind-up, and on my meagre salary couldn't have afforded it in any event, but at home I noticed a virtually empty bottle of scotch from the previous Christmas, so I topped it up with water and colouring, carefully removed a foil top from a new bottle – which was bought ready for visiting aunts and uncles – and put it on my restored one, wrapping it in tissue paper afterwards.

I took it in to work and everyone was hugely embarrassed to think I'd used up my £2 10s weekly wage. One of the gang, George Blackwell (who was slightly merry from the lunchtime drinks in any event) took a whiff, declared it real, and set out glasses for some shots. I started to edge my way out before they took a gulp, but alas I was caught and put inside a storage box that was then nailed up. They did eventually let me out, as you'll have gathered.

Working in the film industry was huge fun – and it sure as heck beat peeling potatoes on a ship! ❏

⌃ My handiwork as a
pavement artist outside the
Tate Gallery.

Early in 1961, when I was a youthful 22 years of age, I'd completed my three-year apprenticeship and was happily contracted to continue in the employment of the Associated British Picture Corporation (ABPC), which I did for a further two years; though I must admit by the end I was eager to spread my wings beyond their increasingly staple fare of low-budget Charlie Drake comedies, and onto some bigger challenges.

As luck would have it, I heard that art director John Box, who was based over at Pinewood, was looking for a draughtsman to go out on location to Jordan for a film about the life of T.E. Lawrence which David Lean was directing. The job carried a wage of £40 a week – regardless of how many hours I worked, he added cautiously – but having started at ABPC on £3, rising to just £15 a week, this new opportunity was quite frankly beyond any of my wildest dreams.

Having secured the job, I gave in my notice at Elstree and flew out to Jordan with two other young art department members – John Graysmark (who had been at MGM Studios Borehamwood beforehand) and Tony Rimmington (from Ealing Studios). Together, I remember us arriving at the Heathrow departure lounge which was actually nothing more glamorous than a long wooden hut with a bar at one end and a large painted mural of the Tower of London at the other. It was certainly nothing like the airport we know today, and was mostly made up of huts and single storey office blocks.

I'd never been to anywhere like Jordan before and, come to think of it, had never stayed in a hotel before either, and so when each morning the call to prayer boomed out from the adjacent mosque I jumped out of bed feeling terribly thrilled that I was being paid to sample the sights and sounds of this magnificent country. Not all of my fellow crew members shared my enthusiasm at being woken up by the disciples of Allah so early each morning.

The film company set up offices in a large mansion, high up overlooking the city of Amman, and I believe it was formerly the Indonesian Embassy. The art department had the first floor, and at lunchtimes all production crew gathered around one long dining table downstairs to be served by Jordanian Army batmen. From my humble beginnings, I now found myself eating lunch with quite possibly the finest

➤ Our director, David Lean (a few years later) posing for a publicity shot.

◄ Peter O'Toole as Lawrence, riding his camel. He actually became very skilled.

British director of his generation, whilst being waited on hand and foot!

During the extensive shoot, the main unit base camp for the large crew was housed on a 67 acre site near the Gulf of Aqaba Docks. There, they had huts, tents and even a beach camp with toilets and showers for the unit to relax after a long day's shoot.

Catering is always one of the most important parts of any location shoot, as without top-notch British based food being served up for the crew, the pos-

sibility of a mutiny was not unheard of. Phil Hobbs (Senior), who'd recently worked with Lean on *Bridge on the River Kwai*, was appointed our caterer for the entire shoot, and soon became known as 'The Conrad Hilton of the desert'. No matter where our furthest outpost, Phil would be there with a makeshift bar and restaurant, thanks to construction manager, Peter Dukelow, and his assistant, Freddy Bennett, serving up favourites such as bangers and mash, steak and kidney pudding and chop and chips; though I did

▲ Footprints in the sand; the first take was always ideal.

of their objective, Pegasus Bridge. To glide in at night, and land so near the mark was hailed by many as the best bit of flying during the war. But I digress ...

My first job on *Lawrence of Arabia* was to measure up and photograph all the railway trucks that we could get hold of, in order to alter them into flak wagons and troop transporters for the railway sabotage scene. I went armed with a new invention, a Polaroid camera. I made the mistake of taking a Polaroid of one of the children hanging around the railway, and giving it to him. I didn't need my Arab translator to work out the calls from a dozen other children of, 'Me! Me! Me!' I returned to the office and explained to the production manager that I'd used up all my expensive film, but I'd made a lot of young friends along the way.

I remember there were a lot of high-level meetings going on with our local liaison, Sir Anthony Nutting, who was quartermaster general of the Jordanian Army. He often spent time at the royal palace with the king, who was taking a great interest in our little project and our many requirements of men, camels and horses.

When someone asked if I'd like to try go-karting down at the airport at the weekend with King Hussein, I was intrigued. I was furthermore told that if I fancied the idea I ought to get friendly with the English girl, Toni Gardener, who worked on the switchboard of our mansion, as she could arrange it. Being rather shy back then, I left it until lunch to make casual conversation, and then a couple of days later, having established a bit of a friendship, I was about to pluck up the courage to ask Toni about the weekend trips out to the airport. When it was noted that this was my third lunch sitting next to Toni, one of the local translators warned me that if I didn't want any trouble, I should 'drop the friendship' because, he added, 'the king has designs on her'.

sometimes wonder if the meat served was always exactly what he professed it to be!

Phil Hobbs became everyone's best friend and, being a Second World War buff, on D-Day matters in particular, it was not until I attended his funeral that I learned Phil was one of the first men to land in Normandy on the night of 5/6 June 1944. He'd co-piloted the second Horsa glider down to within 100ft

I dare say the crew knew that all along, and were sending me up. Sadly, I never did get to go go-karting at the weekend, nor did I share another lunch with that young lady, but I am pleased to say that the king went on to marry her and now their son is the present King Abdullah II of Jordan!

One of the advantages of being the youngest was that I was always told to leave first, and so would get the art department driver to drop me at the hotel. A young, good-looking chap started popping in the office to ask me about the props we were drawing up, from Bedouin tents to canvas buckets. I didn't think too much about him, and just assumed from his daily enquiries that he was a prop man. After a few days he asked if he could catch a lift with me back to the hotel each evening. I was only too happy to oblige. This went on for a while, and I only ever knew him as 'Peter'. Then one evening, he never arrived, so I waited well beyond my usual leaving time and when the driver asked what the problem was I said, 'I'm waiting for Peter the prop guy'.

Well, you may be one step ahead of me by now, but it turned out that Peter was not a prop man at all – he was the star of the film, Peter O'Toole! I'm not *that* daft as to not recognise a star, but at that time he was not an established face. So when he was sent out to Jordan months before our shoot date (unusual for an actor) to acclimatise himself to the desert locations, and to research the Arab history of the story, having never been introduced I didn't really know who he was.

After more meetings between Sir Anthony Nutting and the army it was realised that the 150 camels and 450 horses needed for the charge into Aqaba couldn't all be found in Jordan, so it was decided to transfer a major part of the film to Spain, where they were to spend twelve weeks in Seville before moving over 400km to Almeria. This news, unfortunately, meant that the art department would have to be scaled back in Jordan and, as always, it was 'last in, first out'. So John Graysmark and I left, with a promise they'd take us back on later in the year. Tony Rimmington, meanwhile, had become so immersed in the camel blanket patterns and hundreds of props, that the set dresser Dario Simoni wouldn't let him go.

Our boss, John Box, was very kind in giving us the last two days of our stay off so that we could do a little sightseeing. We travelled to the Dead Sea and took what has now become the obligatory tourist photograph of us sitting in the amazingly buoyant salt water. The next day we headed to Nazareth to visit the Church of the Nativity, inside which was the stable where Jesus was reputedly born. It was all terribly moving – until we emerged only to be swamped by Arab hawkers selling cheap souvenirs and postcards. Talk about shattering the magic of an experience!

On our return from that second day, the driver slammed the back door of the car on poor John's thumb. So swollen and badly crushed was it that the unit nurse back at base told us to go to the local hospital immediately. There, our interpreter bypassed a long queue of people waiting to see the doctor, and within a minute or two the doctor – dressed in a blood-stained green operating gown, having just delivered a baby – appeared and took John off into an office.

When John emerged a short time afterwards he looked terribly pale and said he had to sit down for a few minutes. 'What happened?' I asked.

'That doctor pushed a large fat needle up under my nail to release blood from the swelling,' he replied. I flinched with pain at the very thought of it myself. 'I couldn't scream out. Being English, with all those Arabs in the corridor ...' That was John – he wasn't going to let the side down.

Not only did John become a close friend, I also bought the house next door to him, which proved ideal, as we often worked on the same films and shared a lift into the studios.

I did later receive a call to rejoin the film, but by that time I was working at MGM Studios on a film called *Light in the Piazza* and so, alas, had to decline.

After my shaky start in the precariously uncertain world of a freelancer on *Lawrence*, I returned to Pinewood where perhaps the biggest film of the studio's history was in preparation – *Cleopatra*. I was fortunate to secure a job as draughtsman, and have to say the huge Roman sets on the backlot were very impressive, to say the least. It was on this production that I first met one of my dearest friends, Peter Lamont (who went on to work on eighteen Bond films and win an Oscar for *Titanic*). The sheer vastness of the art department allowed me the opportunity to get

to meet and know lots of other people, which is very valuable when you're always on the lookout for the next job.

Elizabeth Taylor had the title role, and an unheard of million dollar fee. Peter Finch was cast as Caesar, and Stephen Boyd as Mark Antony – though they were later replaced by Rex Harrison and Richard Burton respectively. The distinguished Russian-born director Rouben Mamoulian was hired and spent a year preparing for the task.

Cleopatra was certainly the most expensive and heavily publicised film ever to move into Pinewood. Sets of previously unheard of dimensions were constructed on the backlot. However, soon came the first of the many problems that dogged the production – a shortage of plasterers. The situation became so desperate that the studio finally resorted to advertising on prime-time TV to fill the vacancies.

The most amazing of all the sets was undoubtedly the harbour of Alexandria, which held 1 million gallons of water and was topped up further by the English rain.

▼ A series of photos from the huge set as it was first built at Pinewood (my friend and colleague Peter Lamont appears in the second and third), before it was all packed up and shipped to Rome, where production resumed.

▲ Finally shooting in Rome, and Elizabeth Taylor makes her grand entrance as Cleopatra.

The size of the production was giving cause for concern and, before a foot of film had been exposed, the cost had easily exceeded £1m, and there was still a sixteen week shoot to get underway.

The imminent arrival of 5,000 extras was the next headache. Pinewood's management laid on twenty-eight extra tube trains from London to Uxbridge, and thirty buses to shuttle to and from the station non-stop. Mobile lavatories were hired from Epsom race-course, and massive catering marquees were erected to house the mountain of food for meals. However, all the planning and organisation was wasted – along with all the food– when torrential rain forced shooting to be abandoned.

Then real disaster struck. Elizabeth Taylor became dangerously ill and had to undergo an emergency tracheotomy. Production was halted, and Joan Collins placed on standby as a replacement. Miss Taylor's recuperation was a slow one, and what with the mis-

erable British weather raining down on the sets day after day, the decision was made to transfer production, and Ancient Egypt, to Italy – where the climate was more conducive to Miss Taylor's health. The Pinewood sets were struck and, realising I was unemployed – again – John Graysmark called around one Saturday afternoon to say he'd recommended me for a job with acclaimed production designer Ken Adam: 'They just want someone to travel out to Jamaica, work in the hotel on set drawings and travel back to start the construction at Pinewood a few weeks later.'

I was so excited at the prospect of work, and what's more in the Caribbean, that when the phone rang and

◄ Author Ian Fleming had a home in Jamaica, named 'Goldeneye', and it was quiet convenient for him to pop over and see some filming. Here he is with 007 himself, Sean Connery.

Ken Adam's art director, Syd Cain, started telling me about the location, I just said 'Yes I'm on board'. He laughed, as I think I agreed to the job before he'd actually offered it – but so began my association with James Bond 007.

Dr No was the first of the long-running series and was set to star a relatively unknown actor named Sean Connery. If anyone had said then that they had inkling of an idea just how popular the franchise would become, then I'd say they were lying; as far as we were all concerned it was just a relatively modest budget spy film.

The charter flight out to Jamaica left London on 14 January 1962. Most of the crew, including producer Cubby Broccoli, the lighting cameraman Ted Moore and designer Ken Adam were aboard, whilst director Terence Young and producer Harry Saltzman flew in with Sean Connery a little later.

Our Bristol Britannia, which was more popularly known as the 'Whispering Giant', first stopped off

➤ Director Terence Young chats through a scene with Sean Connery and Ursula Andress.

in Goose Bay, Canada, for refuelling, where the temperature was -32°F and the walk from the plane to the airport lounge literally took your breath away. We then flew on to New York but, before landing, one of the make-up girls fell ill, and broke out in a terrible rash. On the ground, we were all placed into quarantine until a doctor could give the OK for us to leave. Hours passed, and much delayed and exhausted, we were given the all-clear and continued our final leg to Kingston, Jamaica.

The film's budget was fairly tight and so I had to share a room with the stills photographer, Bert Cann, at the Courtleigh Manor Hotel. The rooms were actually more like chalet bungalows and suited our needs admirably. On the first night I heard a woman screaming and immediately jumped up out of my bed to rush to her aid. But, without air conditioning in the rooms and only slatted glass windows for ventilation, we only slept in our underwear and Bert cautioned me not to go outside, 'You'll only end up in more trouble,' he said.

The next morning, we heard that one of the young air hostesses had woken to see a Jamaican man at the window with a long pole, which he'd poked through the glass slats, hooked her handbag and brought it to the window. He had then reached through the glass slats to steal her passport and money from out of it. She said that's when she ran outside to scream for help, and forgot she was just in her bra and knickers. I often think how unfortunate it was that Bert stopped me rushing to her aid!

One of the other chalet rooms doubled up as a makeshift art department, and I used a large sheet of plywood as a drawing board where I was supposed to come up with enough drawings to return to Pinewood, thus enabling Ken to start building sets. Ken, meanwhile, had rented an open top Alfa Romeo sports car and invited me to join him for lunch on a trip down to Port Royal, where Terence Young was staying with his Bond girls. The road down to Port Royal runs parallel with the Norman Manley Airport runway for much of its length, on a narrow spit of land, and so we found ourselves racing a big Boeing down the runway until its take-off point. This was the first time in my life I'd ever been driven at 100mph.

The lunch table was set out with lots of lovely things – as I say, they were all staying there with Terence, and with the hot and humid temperature most were lunching in their swim suits, I might add – and I couldn't help reminding myself I was actually being paid to be there!

On the first Saturday evening we all dined around the hotel pool with a steel band playing dance music. After dinner we were entertained with a fashion show, put on with the help of a bevy of lovely young models, and even a few past 'Miss Jamaicas'. We were royally entertained with evening wear, swimwear and sleepwear. At this point, Sean was asked to choose a girl to start the dance with. He chose Miss Jamaica 1960, and suggested we all take a partner (all still wearing their 'Baby Doll' nightwear) and help him out.

We had a local lad to come and help us. His name was Chris Blackwell and he told me he had his own band. He, of course, went on to form Island Records, working with singers like Bob Marley. Today he's a billionaire and still lives in Jamaica, where he also owns Ian Fleming's former home, 'Goldeneye'.

I didn't spend much time on location as I was busy drawing up Dr No's lair and the reactor room. However, on one occasion I was asked to 'stand by' with the second unit on the twisting mountain road that Bond is chased down by a hearse full of assassins. I had to build a camera hide down a slope from the road, for the hearse to crash towards. I realised that the weight of the vehicle, coming down a 45 degree slope, would need something more than I could build around the hide to stop it being demolished, should the car hit it. So with the help of a lot of railway sleepers, the construction gang built it on top of a gully running down. We were pretty confident that, if the hearse left the road at the correct spot, it would be trapped in the gulley to continue the driverless journey down to the bottom of the mountain.

When I assured the camera boys that the hide was perfectly safe, they said, 'Well you won't mind joining us in there then will you?' With my fingers crossed, I stood behind the camera with the operator and focus puller and watched the hearse go down through the gulley, just as I'd hoped – thank goodness.

All too soon it was time to leave our Caribbean paradise and, with a two day stopover in New York, I boarded the plane for home. Somehow or other I managed to lose my wallet, and without much spending money for my weekend in the Big Apple, I walked

▲ This is where it all started – with Ian Fleming's books. *Thunderball* was originally going to be the first film, but legal complications saw the producers choose *Dr No* instead.

▲ Director, Terence Young, and producer, Cubby Broccoli, on location at Port Royal in Jamaica.

everywhere. From 42nd street I walked the forty blocks south to catch a ferry to the Statue of Liberty. In those days, you could climb up a very narrow and tight circular stairway to the top of her arm and to the balcony around the flame, then down the other side. I don't remember how many steps I climbed, but they went on and on and on until … darkness. Only then did I realise my head was partly up the black dress of the slower lady in front of me. I think I just about got away with a big apology!

I ate very cheaply too, counting my loose change out at diners, but I do think I got to see more of New York than anyone else did in just a couple of days.

Back at Pinewood, I was asked to go on the set of Bond's apartment, where I was confronted by the lovely Eunice Gayson wearing only a man's white shirt covering a pair of knickers. I was dumbstruck, and with my jaw firmly on the ground couldn't even say 'good morning'. I delivered my message and left. It was quite a daring appearance for a leading actress in a film, because up until then if a lady showed a little too much shoulder or leg there were calls for it to be reshot. But *Dr No* changed all that, with its fantastic blend of escapism, beautiful ladies and exotic locations and I'm sure many men of my generation said 'hallelujah to that'!

Dissolve to fifty years later, and again at Pinewood Studios. I was invited to join 150 other people at the '50 Years of Bond' lunch and I, along with Peter Lamont, found myself on the top table with Sir Roger Moore, Honor Blackman and Eunice Gayson – with whom I chatted non-stop throughout the afternoon. I guess I'm no longer that shy 20-something any more.

Dr No's underground reception area had a large glass wall which was to depict an underwater scene, and that footage was shot in the Bahamas, though I guess the guys who filmed it were just told to capture some fish on film, as the fish were so close to the lens that they looked like giant sharks. Unsure as to what to do with it, disaster was averted when someone came up with the idea of putting an extra line in the script saying the image is magnified 'making minnows look like whales'. That was also the set where Bond spots the famous Goya portrait of the Duke of Wellington, which had recently been stolen from the National Gallery.

Johanna Harwood, the screenwriter, came up with the idea when they came to look at the set on a Friday – and needed it in place for Monday. That job fell to Ron Quelch, who was the buyer on the film, and he rushed over to the National Gallery, purchased a postcard of the painting and took it to a company somewhere south of the river to enlarge it onto canvas on Saturday morning. When Ron went to collect it in the afternoon he found the enlarging process had softened the image and rang Ken Adam, who told him to drop it in to his house in Knightsbridge. Ken worked on it over the weekend, and at 8 a.m. on Monday morning the portrait was nicely displayed on set – and nobody knew how we did it so quickly.

I only ever saw Bond's creator, Ian Fleming, on set once at Pinewood, and that was for the reactor room

◄ The first lady of Bond (and one I was too tongue-tied to speak to!), Eunice Gayson wearing the famous red dress as Sylvia Trench.

finale. He seemed terribly impressed by the set, or at least was kind enough to say he was.

Of course the success of *Dr No* led to *From Russia with Love* being swung into production the following year and my association with Bond continued, on and off, through to *Casino Royale* in 2006. ❏

3 *Summer Holiday* (1962)

FILM CREDITS

Summer Holiday

Director: Peter Yates

Stars: Cliff Richard,
Lauri Peters, Melvyn Hayes

I had worked with Peter Yates a few times during my five years at Elstree Studios when he was a first assistant director, so it was very nice to return to my parent studio as a freelancer and have him as my director on this movie.

With the success of Cliff Richard's third film, *The Young Ones*, it was inevitable that another film with a few more ambitious locations would be on the cards. This was Peter's first film as director, and from those early beginnings he went on to direct *Bullitt* with Steve McQueen in America, and won much praise for the iconic car chase he staged in San Francisco. It's always nice to see people you know climb the ladder, especially in the fickle world of film.

The first job the designer, Syd Cain, gave me was to produce working plans to build the inside of a double-decker London Transport RT-type bus, the forerunner to the Routemaster. The London Transport centre for repairs and overhauls in Aldenham was very close to the studios, so I arranged a visit to order all the interior fittings, bell pushes, handles and complete window assemblies. Our script, by the way, called for a bus to

➤ Going for a take.

➤➤ When a little elevation is required …

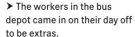
➤ The workers in the bus depot came in on their day off to be extras.

be converted into a mobile home. The scenes with Cliff and his fellow mechanics altering the interior were all shot at Aldenham during the summer shutdown, and a lot of the mechanics came in to portray extras working in the background. The whole song 'Seven Days to a Holiday' was written around these scenes.

My father had bought a Dormobile, the English equivalent of the Volkswagen camper van, so I was not a stranger to knowing the best way to utilise small spaces for fold-out tables, storage units and shower facilities, etc. It was great fun to fit it out with the upper deck as the sleeping area, though we only saw it a very few times in the final film.

We prepared three identical buses; two were shipped out to Greece, as it was felt that to drive them the 1,500 miles would be very risky for two old vehicles, not even taking into account the low bridge problems en route. The third bus did drive over as far as France for the shots in Paris.

As we had a very tight budget and schedule we couldn't afford the luxury of filming the bus out and about on the streets, so, to achieve the movement effect (against back projection of locations) we mounted the interior (lower deck) set on giant tractor inner tubes and had the standby stagehands rocking it gently up and down. Not the most sophisticated method to represent movement, I must admit, especially as they tended to overdo it most of the time.

For one of the biggest scenes of the movie, Cliff was driving whilst singing the title song. Disaster struck when the gearbox under the steering column broke free. To keep the cameras turning, John Graysmark and myself crawled under the rostrum and held up the metal support, enabling Cliff to complete what was needed. As you can imagine, every time I hear him sing 'We're all going on a summer holiday' I think back to being under the bus holding it all together!

One Saturday, John Graysmark and I were working on a small stage on which one of the buses was parked. John climbed in and pressed the start button; the engine fired and John drove it a few feet forward then, engaging reverse, brought it back to its original

∧ Lovely Peter Yates, our director, chatting with Cliff Richard.

position, and asked me 'how do you stop it?' Well, I had no idea, but the stage quickly began filling with blue exhaust fumes. John started panicking that we'd land up in real trouble. I dashed out and eventually found a mechanic, and he came over to save the day. He just revved the engine, lifted his foot off the accelerator and then lifted the pedal up beyond its natural stop with his foot placed under it. At last the engine cut out and, more importantly, the stage stopped filling up with blue smoke. We managed to find the switch to open the big stage doors and get some fresh air in to help hide the evidence of our meddling with things we really did not understand.

In my fifty years in the film industry I have only been invited to attend two premieres, *Summer Holiday* being the first. I arrived in Leicester Square about an hour before the start time on the tickets, only to be confronted with a wall of people at least 150 yards from the cinema. It was fast becoming a dangerous situation, as everyone was pushing to get near the front of the cinema in the hope of seeing Cliff Richard arrive. The big guys at the entrance called out, 'Anyone with tickets fight your way through', which was easier said than done!

The thought of waving my tickets in the air and having someone grab them made me want to keep

➤ He went that way!

➤➤ The cast, minus Cliff Richard, in the bus. Ding-ding!

▼ Una Stubbs, Melvyn Hayes, Cliff Richard and Lauri Peters.

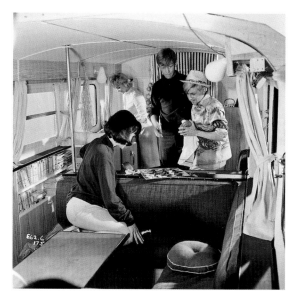

them in my inside pocket, but as I had the folded A4 note that came with them, I held this aloft and slowly fought my way through the masses with my wife hanging on to my coat for all she was worth. Finally, I was in front of one of the big guys and pulled my tickets out to show him. As he suspiciously looked me up and down, a stuntman I had worked with on an earlier film came across to say hello and we were quickly ushered in. I felt he had saved us from a frightening crushing machine when we finally made it to the tranquillity of the cinema foyer. As you can imagine, my hunger to attend premieres after that experience waned somewhat. ❑

4 *The Moon-Spinners* (1963)

Having just completed my second James Bond film, *From Russia with Love*, I was asked by Tony Masters (one of our top film designers) to join him for a film in Crete. It was to star Hayley Mills, Joan Greenwood and Eli Wallach.

The Moon-Spinners was Disney's attempt at easing their child protégée into adulthood. It was a romantic thriller in which Hayley finally landed her first screen kiss – and it was from the handsome young Peter McEnery.

We had to build a whole fishing village on the beach with a run of six houses leading to a hotel with its own jetty into the sea. We also needed to build a practical Greek windmill for shooting both inside and out.

I promise you, every van and bicycle around that little Greek village had stickers declaring it was part of the 'Walt Disney Productions' team. We thought the printer in the nearby larger town of Agios Nikolaos was selling the stickers to everyone as we were sure we couldn't have had that amount of people working for us!

FILM CREDITS

The Moon-Spinners
(Assistant Art Director)
Director: James Neilson
Stars: Hayley Mills,
Eli Wallach, Pola Negri

◀ Our star, Hayley Mills.

➤ Here, I am working on an art department model of a windmill in Crete. The drawing on the wall behind is the fishermen's village that we later built.

➤➤ We built this entrance to the Moon-Spinners Hotel.

Our location base for the big set-build was Elounda, with the old leper colony on the island of Spinalonga a short distance off the shore. I was left in the office on one particular morning, drawing up the wrought iron panels for the front entrance to the Moon-Spinners Hotel, whilst the rest of the crew were out on various location work, when my office door opened and the 'big man' himself walked in, Mr Disney. He was alone, and had noticed my 'Art Department' sign on this fisherman's cottage on the beach front and just popped in.

I made him a coffee and we chatted for about twenty-five minutes. I told him about the progress in building the village, and showed him Tony Masters' sketches along with my drawing of the exterior of the hotel set. He was the most affable, charming and interesting man you could ever hope to meet, and totally unassuming.

I found out many years later that he made a habit of just turning up unannounced, to quietly walk around and talk to the construction crew without the produc-tion team rolling out the red carpet and organising a formal guided tour – he liked to see things for himself.

Thirty-two years later, me and *101 Dalmatians* designer Assheton Gorton were asked to go over to Florida's Disneyland and view the special exhibition they had built to publicise the film, which included a facsimile of both our offices. On our final day, we were asked to take part in a Q & A session with Disney's top designers and staff. It was a pretty daunting prospect, and I rightly assumed that my boss, Assheton, would take the lead, but he started by saying that I was more adept at answering any questions, and promptly sat back down! Not knowing what was about to be fired at me, I was hugely relieved to be asked by one of the senior secretaries, 'I'm told you once met and chatted with Walt Disney. What was he like, and what did you ask him?' Well, that was easy to answer, and the fact that I had, in their eyes, actually met 'God', impressed the most hard-nosed members of the group more than any answer to a complicated technical question of filming 101 puppies would have!

Back on location for *The Moon-Spinners*, I remember – after a very stormy night – I was asked by John Stears, our special effects supervisor, to help him take a very colourful *caique* fishing boat from the Agios Nikolaos Harbour around the headland to a location 2 miles along the coast. The actual bay we were to end up in was very rocky, so our construction manager, Gus Walker, had built a jetty from scaffolding and timber for us to tie up to. However – and unbeknown to us until we arrived – the storm had completely wrecked the jetty. Realising the scenes involving the boat were scheduled for the next morning, John asked if I would dive overboard and take two lines – one from the bow and the other from the stern – to keep it from smashing up on the rocks. Luckily I was a good swimmer.

As I was, in my mind, performing actions well above the call of duty, I felt very disappointed when, after an hour or so, John changed his mind and said, 'we can't risk leaving it here, in case another storm blows up in the night'. So, all my saving-the-day heroics went out the window. We finally beached it in a sandy bay close by, in the hope that the camera boat could pull us off the sand in the morning.

Building the Greek windmill was another interesting job. Unlike English windmills, these have cloth sails, which can be furled or unfurled according to the wind. I drew up the design from Tony Masters' sketch, and inside it we had a big axle fixed into two free-wheeling bearings. We then fitted the cloth sails, and on releasing the brake it actually started to go around. The pleasure we got from seeing it revolve was no less than Wilber Wright might have had witnessing his brother take to the skies for the first time, I am sure.

The interior of our windmill was to be built back in the studio at Pinewood, so I had to photograph and make a detailed study of the real giant wooden wheels and cogs that formed the mechanism for grinding the

corn. I was halfway into the drawing when we learned from a local that a farmer had an old windmill that had been derelict for ten years, but the timber grinding wheel was still intact. The Greek production manager did a deal to purchase the bits we needed, saving me the job of replicating them.

Off we went to the farm in the next valley to get a tubular rig made, to which we could attach a block and tackle to lower the big wheels to ground level. It really was a coup. However hard we would have tried to make our own wheels and cogs look authentic, we would never have had the wonderful bleached and worn look that those original pieces had. The wheels stayed in the Pinewood scene dock for years until they cleared it out for more workshop space.

▲ Ready to shoot at the windmills.

Meanwhile, the 1936 Rolls-Royce hearse that we had shipped out from England had arrived in the docks at Heraklion, so I drove over to measure it up for some decorative additions. Tony wanted to make it more fitting for a Greek funeral and not looking 'too English' in its appearance. I had seen the hearse prior to it being shipped, and at that time I had noticed a rather macabre item in the back – a false leg. I did not want to contemplate what it was doing there, but after its long sea voyage I couldn't believe the leg was still there – not even the customs men dared examine it for smuggled diamonds or drugs!

I'm never one to sit around and just enjoy time off, so when our caterer mentioned he was a waterskiing enthusiast, I asked if he might teach me the rudimentary skills of the sport. Each evening and weekend he took me out to watch him practising his jumps and spins, and then suggested I have a go. He also offered to give Hayley Mills some lessons, and it wasn't long before we were both being pulled around the bay side-by-side. Suddenly, though, she stopped coming, and we realised her mother (Mary Hayley-Bell) had banned her from doing any more, as she thought it was too dangerous. On reflection, with so much at stake with her Disney contract, she was probably right. ❏

5 *The Heroes of Telemark* (1964)

This was another true story from the Second World War, and centred on the destruction of a factory producing 'heavy water', which could, in turn, have enabled Hitler to construct an atomic bomb. As it was only twenty-one years after the event, we were fortunate to enlist the help of Knut Haukelid, who became our technical advisor; he was a Special Operations Executive trained commando who took part in the original raid on the hydro factory above the Norwegian town of Rhukan. Richard Harris played Knut's part in the film, whilst Kirk Douglas played the part of a local physics professor, Rolf Pederson.

In 1964 the hydro factory was still producing the fertiliser from which the heavy water had been drawn, two decades earlier. Very little had changed. Apart from adding the outer security fencing topped with barbed wire, the art department had a small amount to do to recreate its wartime appearance. In fact,

FILM CREDITS

The Heroes of Telemark (Assistant Art Director)
Director: Anthony Mann
Stars: Kirk Douglas, Richard Harris, Ulla Jacobsson

◄ Kirk Douglas and Richard Harris – it's difficult to believe they didn't get on very well during the shoot.

As the town was always in the shade of the mountains in winter, local children were allowed to ride for free in the cable cars to get some sun!

erecting the fencing was easy as the Norwegian construction team just dug holes in the hard-packed snow, dropped the posts in and, having secured them in the upright position, poured cold water into the holes. With temperatures well below freezing the water set like concrete in just a few hours.

The entrance to the factory was over a narrow road bridge that spanned a deep ravine, and it was decided to build a German pillbox at the turn-off to the bridge. Tony Masters, my production designer, indicated where he wanted it erected, and my job was to find a photo of a six-sided pillbox and produce drawings for the new construction. With drawings in hand, I pointed out the position Tony had previously shown me. The local crew started to dig out a flat area into the bank at the junction of the two roads. Later that day I had a message to go and visit the site before they put together the pieces of the pillbox. As I arrived I noticed a lot of smiling, friendly, grinning faces, which I thought was unusual, as they'd been out for hours digging in the extreme cold. It turned out that they'd uncovered, in exactly the same position, the six-sided concrete base of a pillbox covered over with dirt, which had been hidden away since the war!

The script called for a big rock, about the size of a van, to be rolled down the mountain in an attempt to kill Reichskommissar Terboven, who was paying a visit to the heavy water factory. The boulder was constructed at Pinewood Studios from fibreglass moulded to fit over a substantial metal frame. Once finished, it was loaded onto a lorry and driven to Norway. Having overcome a low bridge en route by letting its tyres down to enable it to just scrape underneath, we finally unloaded it and pulled it up the side of the mountain by connecting a wire to the inner frame and winching it up above the road along which Terboven's convoy would drive.

To protect the town below, a large net was constructed on the far side of the road, out of picture, to catch and stop the dummy rock from rolling any further. On the actual take, as our band of heroes levered the boulder free, this was timed with the cutting of the safety wire. It rolled down the mountain, gathering speed, and the fibreglass construction turned it into a giant ping-pong ball. When it hit the road it bounced and cleared the safety net, heading on towards the town, though thankfully, the only damage done was when it crushed someone's potting shed before coming to a stop.

Our local interpreter was Gunn Sorensen, and we learned that her father was the captain of the hydro ferry that was sunk by the saboteurs in 1943, destroying the remaining heavy water being shipped out to Germany. It's always very special to meet the real heroes of a story you are retelling, and for me meeting Gunn's father, Erling, was one of the things I'll remember forever.

The other was meeting Knut Haukelid, who became our main technical adviser.

Our location set dresser, Ted Clements, purchased four types of wire cutters in London for the scene in which our heroes slip through the fence. He thought he would let Knut make a final choice – after all he was there! When Knut turned all of them down, Ted decided he would buy some others locally, enquired where the best tool shop was, and explained he needed a good selection to choose from. From that one enquiry he discovered that Knut's original wire cutters had been found by the outer fence the next morning, and kept as a souvenir ever since. Having been able to obtain them, Ted slipped them in with the three he'd bought and was amazed when Knut passed the original over, choosing a smaller pair. When Ted confessed to his ruse,

▲ Rhukan town square, dressed ready for filming.

Knut said he couldn't remember after twenty-one years! In all fairness Knut was very helpful to us in getting the film to look historically correct in all its other aspects.

The worst part of the shoot was undoubtedly filming the Christmas sequence in the local church. We brought in a very large Christmas tree covered in lights, and every light bulb in the building was switched on to supplement our generator-fed studio lamps. At the end of the day with all shots in the can, the crew left, and the church was locked up for the night. But it seemed that the old wiring, fixed in the eaves, was so overloaded it must have been glowing red towards the end of our shoot. It was then, when we opened the big church doors to leave, that the wind from outside came in and fanned the glow into flames which, in turn, caught the old dried timbers of the roof. A few hours later, in the middle of the night, the whole of this ancient church – which had survived

RJUKAN
UNDER
CLOUD

▲ And the low cloud doesn't help matters, either …

THE STRANGEST MISSION OF SABOTAGE UNDER THE MIDNIGHT SUN!

COLUMBIA PICTURES presents
A Benton Film Production

KIRK **DOUGLAS** · RICHARD **HARRIS**

IN ANTHONY MANN'S

THE HEROES OF TELEMARK

PANAVISION® COLUMBIACOLOR

Co-starring ULLA JACOBSSON · MICHAEL REDGRAVE with DAVID WESTON · ANTON DIFFRING Screenplay by IVAN MOFFAT and BEN BARZMAN Produced by S. BENJAMIN FISZ Directed by ANTHONY MANN

the worst of the Second World War – was now ablaze, thanks to a British film crew!

We rescheduled the next day's shoot high up on a plateau away from the townspeople, who were naturally very upset with us all for burning down their church and the historic artefacts within, though the company readily agreed to pay for the restoration.

We upset the locals on another occasion, too. All of our young extras were naturally kitted out in full Nazi uniform, but on a break between scenes some extras decided to go into the town, forgetting about their outfits. Most of the older townspeople, who had suffered so terribly during the war, no doubt wished the film crew would leave and not return, seeing them in the town must have brought back all their bad memories.

Back in the factory, we were allowed to shoot in the actual room containing the electrolysis chambers, where the charges were placed in 1943. We therefore had to prepare some dummy chambers in lead, all cut and bent out of shape, to add in place of the originals, in order to show the damage done after the explosion.

The final scenes were the blowing up of the ferry containing the tankers, supposedly full of heavy water. As we couldn't sink the real ferry (destroying their church was bad enough!) crossing the Tinnsjo Lake, we built a large 1/5 size model, together with model rail tankers to roll off into the lake. Not wanting to lose the expensive model, the special effects team rigged some air bags that, when inflated, would bring it back to the surface again. Sadly, our best laid plans did not work out as the model ferry boat sank to the

◄ The pillbox we built, leading to the factory bridge.

bottom of the very deep lake and was never seen again. I often wondered how far away the 'baby' was from its bigger 'mother' which had sunk there twenty years earlier.

On the last weekend of location work Jack Maxstead, the art director, arranged for a thirty-seater coach to take some of our local crew up to a mountaintop restaurant where there was a dance with a live band every Saturday night. The general format was for the guys to bring soft drink bottles laced with their homemade hooch to pass around, since the whole of the area was alcohol-free. I certainly saw more people the worse for wear at the dance than you would have if alcohol had been freely available at the bar!

Anyhow, as the road zigzagged around the mountain, we looked down into a deep ravine that formed a perpendicular drop from the road and was only occasionally protected by sparsely-spaced safety barriers. Just then, a fierce snowstorm began and the coach found the road very difficult with the steep gradients, especially on the hairpin bends. With progressively worsening road conditions, we skidded to a stop with the rear nearside wheels dangerously close to going off the road. For safety, we were all asked by the driver to exit the bus whilst he struggled to fit the vehicle's rear snowchains on. As there was not one umbrella between us, it wasn't long before all the girls were wearing little white snow hats on their backcombed bouffant hairstyles, which were all the rage at that time. The below-zero winds just blew through the piled-up hair and kept the snow from melting. Twenty minutes later, the driver said it was now safe to re-enter the coach and we started off again, and, with the ladies' 'snow hats' soon melting, all the clever hairstyling proceeded to collapse over their faces. The girls were naturally upset, but the guys could see the funny side of it. If only digital cameras had been available then to record that moment!

We finally arrived at the mountaintop restaurant and the girls went off to do some hurried beauty repairs to their hair. A good end of picture dinner, with lots of special soft drink bottles, was our way of thanking all the locals who had been so helpful and friendly with us during our invasion of their town in mid-winter. ❏

6 *2001: A Space Odyssey* (1968)

FILM CREDITS

2001: A Space Odyssey
Director: Stanley Kubrick
Stars: Keir Dullea, Gary
Lockwood, William Sylvester

I suppose out of all the films I've worked on, taking the designer's ideas and transforming them into working drawings, Stanley Kubrick's *2001: A Space Odyssey* must rank as the number one in terms of challenges, workload and sheer vision.

I read an account Stanley gave after the film was released, where he said he strove to make the sets, models and visual effects the stars of the film. I guess he was right, because if questioned upon which actors starred in the film, I'm sure most people would be hard-pressed to remember. However, most would still remember all the hardware and, in particular, the scenes where we approach the space station, over which the haunting notes of Johann Strauss the

> Our director, Stanley Kubrick was certainly a taskmaster, and had little concept of normal working hours or rest days. Oscar-winning production designer, Sir Ken Adam, later said of him, 'Such is my love and admiration for Stanley that I will never work with him again!'

Younger's best known waltz, '*An Der Schönen Blauen Donau*' ('On the beautiful Blue Danube'), play out.

I bumped into Stanley in a record shop in Borehamwood High Street some months after we had finished filming, and noticed he was buying a selection of classical albums. I often wondered if Johann Strauss and Richard Strauss's albums were amongst earlier buys from that same store?

Stanley was a perfectionist in all things. Before he even made contact with Arthur C. Clark he had viewed every 'journey into space' type movie he could lay his hands on, and having seen some (low budget ones) from the 1950s and 1960s Stanley realised that none of them portrayed the believability and realism that he knew he could bring to his film.

In 1964 Stanley received the 'Best Director of the Year' award from the New York critics (for *Dr Strangelove*). This gave him the extra clout he needed to get his space film moving, and in April of that year he met up with author Arthur C. Clark in Trader Vics at the Plaza Hotel in New York to secure the rights (at this time Stanley was still living in the Big Apple, prior to moving to England full-time). Its original title was announced by MGM as 'Journey to the Stars', without Stanley knowing. He later changed it to the one we all know!

Today, nearly five decades later, the film still holds up and, when you think that's set against productions of recent years with the benefit of multi-million dollar digital imaging techniques, it really does say a lot about Stanley's sharp eye for perfection.

The three main sets I was tasked with were the 'hotel bedroom', the 'Pod Bay of Discovery' and the 'Centrifuge'. Completing a series of construction

The bedroom set, with Stanley Kubrick operating the camera. He was a perfectionist when it came to getting the exact shot he wanted.

▲ A photograph taken by Stanley Kubrick of the art department at work. He later presented it to me. John Graysmark, Tony Reading, John Fenner and me.

drawings for the Centrifuge alone became a five months' exercise; it was a giant 30 ton revolving metal wheel 38ft in diameter in which the set was to be housed. Vickers Armstrong built the framework and the supporting legs. The foundations for the four legs, incidentally, had to be dug down 5ft below the studio floor – with a promise to reinstate it on completion. I remember seeing the men digging out pure London clay that had lain thirty years under the stage and was still moist enough to use as modelling clay.

The Centrifuge had to cater for all the necessary elements to allow two men to live in space for eighteen months, plus three crew who were put into hibernation. The areas on both sides, radiating from the centre axle, were designed as kitchen, dining and washing facilities along with work stations. The two adjustable sleeping benches, meanwhile, were close

to the three hibernating crew members. Stanley had all the latest information on space travel coming into him from NASA, via two men he brought onto the payroll – Fred Ordway and a brilliant conceptual artist, Harry Lange. Stanley was put in touch with them by Arthur C. Clark.

We learned that the technology was available to put a human into a state of hibernation to preserve life, without using up vital food and oxygen supplies, on the long voyage to Jupiter for our scenario. We were told that a human's heartbeat would need to be reduced to a much lower rate to, in turn, reduce the body's metabolism and energy consumption. I read lots of research pamphlets on the subject and found out, to the amusement of the other set designers in the office, that the one thing the body will not reduce is the continual production of sperm. 'Will the hiber-

nating crew members have to be "relieved" on the eighteen months voyage to Jupiter?' was the question that followed!

The glass-topped hibernacula (the self-contained chambers where an astronaut could sleep for months, potentially) were one of the few things that did not change from their original design.

The lighting had to be integrated into the set, and Stanley insisted that all the buttons were practical and the twenty-four TV monitors with attached film projectors were all able to work when required. So you can imagine, outside this giant 'hamster wheel' were an array of spaghetti-like electrical feeds all going into the centre axle connecting to the revolving electrical brush pick-ups.

Shooting in a giant wheel gave us many problems, and overcoming them with Stanley's continual 'input'

was always a challenge, but love him or loathe him, you always put in your best work. To keep up with all the changes warranted every weekend, Tony Masters, our production designer, asked us all to work both Saturday and Sunday. I remember, after six weeks without a day off, I tried to hide on Friday afternoons when we had to commit to coming in or not. Draughtsmen who promised to come in when it was a sunny weekend were very few and far between. I was then put in with a night gang to work on the changes and additions of the day, just to keep ahead of Stanley's infinite requirements!

One thing that caught us out were the rubber mats covering the floor of the Centrifuge. John Hoesli (assistant art director) had found a company to cast them to our design, which facilitated a fixed camera to slot through the centre line of the set on a gap of 5mm.

▲ The 30 ton wheel structure of the centrifuge set. This was used to simulate gravity by virtue of the centripetal force generated by its rotation at the heart interior of the spaceship, *Discovery*.

▲▲ The 'Moon Rocket Bus' set under construction on the MGM stage.

The camera was mounted to stay put as the drum revolved around it. John carefully took the exact radius of the plywood floor which was divided up into 'two mat-length doors' that hinged down for access to any part of the Centrifuge. Having then arrived at the total circumference, he divided by fifty-two to give us twenty-six doors around the circumference, each side of the slot.

The mats arrived at the studio with the odd length of 'x' plus 9/32in – this was to give us a tight butt finish so a fixed camera dolly could roll around the revolving wheel. No one took into consideration that the plywood between the fixing ribs was straight, and therefore a minute amount was gained on each rib. Take that around the whole circumference and it amounted to a more than 1in overlap of the last two mats. Knowing how Stanley was so meticulous for detail we had to shave a little off half the mats to form an unbroken matching fit.

NASA obviously knew about the film, and a small delegation came over from the States to see our Centrifuge. It was well known that, for long journeys in space, some form of gravity would be needed for the astronauts to avoid problems connected with excessive weightlessness, and the best way would be in a revolving drum spinning at a given rate to give artificial 'earth-like gravity'. The NASA team were frankly amazed at our Centrifuge and sets, but when Stanley showed them the filmed sequence of the air hostess walking up the wall of the Orion spaceship with her grip shoes, and exiting the set upside down, they just

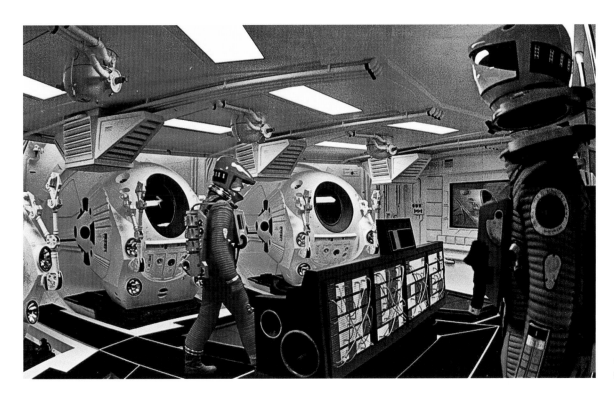

◄ The pod bay – one of the sets I drew up.

could not understand how we'd somehow conquered weightless conditions without boarding a plane or a spacecraft. Equally impressive is the shot of Dr Frank Poole, one of the astronauts, jogging to keep fit around the Centrifuge wheel with the fixed camera following him for a full circle. Even when viewed on the computer now, it's difficult to appreciate his jogging feet are always facing the stage floor.

Since we were designing hardware that was thirty-three years into the future, some of the ideas were pure conjecture, though now they are part of every-day life. See the scene, for instance, where our astro-naut has a small handheld TV screen with computer information displayed very much like tablets today.

Arthur C. Clark was writing about communica-tion satellites way back in 1945, and how TV and telephone companies would be making huge profits

from these orbiting satellites. He gave to the film all his knowledge of how it would be possible to trans-mit telephone calls from Earth to a moon base or space station.

The movie remains a landmark of design, with its groundbreaking in-camera effects, pioneered by Wally Veevers, who was the frontrunner in mul-tiple split-screen exposures and matting techniques (where he sometimes ran the same film through the camera many times, exposing different areas to create a whole negative).

The film sadly only won one Oscar for visual effects, with best film going to Carol Reed's *Oliver* that year. However, for the 1969 BAFTA Awards the art direction won, along with Geoffrey Unsworth's best cinematog-raphy and best soundtrack. I attended the event held at London's Albert Hall, and two seats along from me were reserved for Stanley and his wife. I was a bit nervous as to what I would say for the duration of the event, but Stanley never showed up. It was a pity, since his input had helped each of the three winning categories to achieve their award success.

Unfortunately, very little remains of the hundreds of drawings we did, as Stanley ordered them all to be destroyed, along with the models and sets on completion of the film. Now, forty-six years later, I'm left with only the memories of that incredible year, and am proud to have worked on that amazing movie. ❏

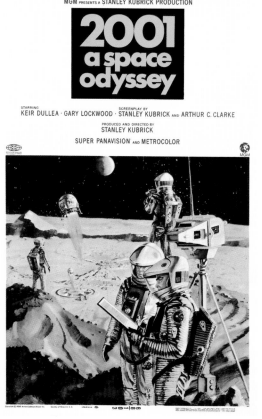

7 *Battle of Britain* (1969)

I have always been interested in the Second World War, no doubt because I lived through it having been born just seven months before Hitler's army invaded Poland on 1 September 1939.

With my father away serving in Burma, I was evacuated, with my mother, away from the London Blitz and to the relative safety of her cousin's house in Lancing, West Sussex. This was an interesting move, I've always felt, given that the south coast was the closest point to the German forces at the time. After my mother's death in 2006, I found a letter she'd written to my father from Lancing, saying 'Alan is always running in from the garden to tell me the names of the planes that were flying over. I don't know how he recognises one from the other.'

My ability to recognise one from the other, and indeed my continuing fascination with old war planes, has served me particularly well in my career, not least when I was asked if I'd be interested in working on Guy Hamilton's film, *Battle of Britain*. They didn't have to ask twice!

No sooner had I joined the production than we were laid off for a couple of months, probably due to the producer Harry Saltzman needing more time to tie

FILM CREDITS

Battle of Britain
Director: Guy Hamilton
Stars: Michael Caine, Trevor Howard

◄ The first day of filming in Spain, at Iruzan. Goering alights from his train.

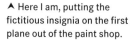
⌃ Here I am, putting the fictitious insignia on the first plane out of the paint shop.

up the finance, and when we all returned I was put in charge of the camouflage and markings of the British planes. With that job done, I dashed off to Spain to do the same with the Heinkel bombers and Bouchon Me 109s which, in 1968, made up the majority of the Spanish air force. We painted-up thirty-two Heinkels and seventeen Messerschmitts in all.

The producers then faced a dilemma: should they use fictitious squadron code letters, or try and represent the actual real ones? Given that the task of portraying every squadron absolutely accurately in a film which, let's face it, always has to embellish a little, would prove an enormous extra burden (and one the producers didn't need); it also risked upsetting the pilots and their families if we got it wrong. So I was asked to produce a list of markings that had never been used in the conflict. Thankfully, our advisor, John Blake, helped me out. He was employed to primarily design the fighter and bomber formations, and to give advice on our storyboards

which, in turn, guided the aerial unit director and pilots as to what was required by the camera before they took off.

For the Spitfires, 'A1', 'B0', 'CD', 'D0', 'E1', 'EQ' and 'LC' were selected. The Hurricanes, meanwhile, which were mainly used in the 'fall of France' sequence at the beginning of the film, had another fictitious set, with the one exception being Keith Parks' plane, which bore the authentic letters 'OK-1' and was used in scenes where Park (played by Trevor Howard) flies into Hawkinge and later Northolt for top-level meetings with Leigh-Mallory (Patrick Wymark) and Dowding (Laurence Olivier). All the codes were stuck on by the Scotch-3M company, who guaranteed their sticky-backed 'Fablon' wouldn't blow away during our dogfights. Of course, as we had limited Spitfires, we had to change the squadron codes and identity serial numbers many times to give the impression of infinitely more planes being involved, and never have I been so grateful for sticky-backed letters.

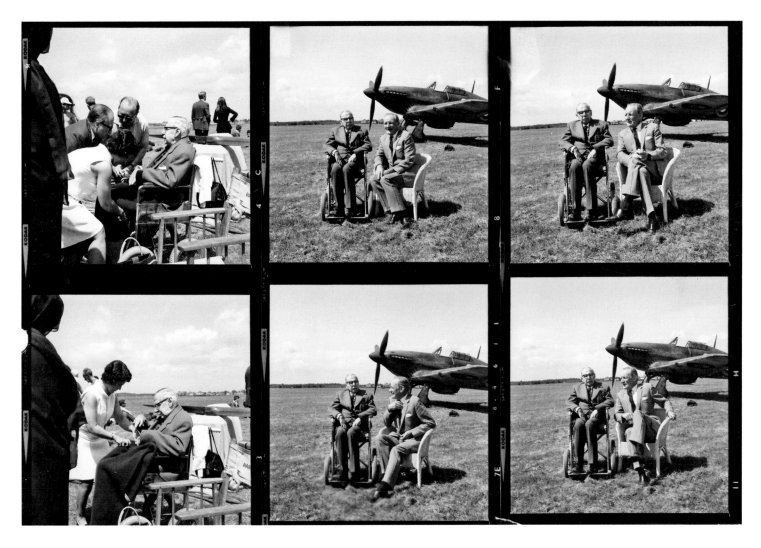

Many years after the film came out, a lot of air-to-air colour footage ended up in various film stock libraries, and you often see the clips slipped in to factual documentaries – I guess I'm one of the few people who'd know it was actually shot in 1968 and not 1940!

The A1 Squadron code was Michael Caine's in the movie, and probably had the most coverage throughout, so I was especially pleased when Dinky Toys pro-

duced a Spitfire II model with A1-A on it, coinciding with the film's release the following year.

The film's construction crew all arrived in Spain in January 1968 and, shortly after, I headed down to the Huelva Sand Dunes on a recce. This whole beach area is located between Seville and the Portuguese border – but only later did I discover it was the exact same place where 'the man who never was' washed ashore in 1943, in a wartime deception tactic by the Allies to

⋏ Trevor Howard with the real life hero of the battle, Lord Dowding, who visited us on set.

BATTLE OF BRITAIN FILM MODELS FEATURE

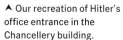
▲ Our recreation of Hitler's office entrance in the Chancellery building.

▲▲ Who says we don't have fun on films? Here we are, blowing up the central hangar at Duxford during the airfield bombing scenes.

➤ These are some of the radio-controlled models built for the film under the supervision of John Sidall and Jack Morton.

fool Hitler with false information about the invasion (a film was made in 1955 starring Clifton Webb).

Anyhow, roll on nearly two decades and I found myself back in the area again looking for locations for David Lean's *Nostromo.* It was whilst I was there that I was asked to find the grave of that anonymous body for my friend Winston Ramsey, editor of *After the Battle* magazine. I found it, photographed it, and was pleased to see it actually made the cover of the publication. My first magazine cover.

Meanwhile, back in 1968, the location of the sand dunes doubled admirably for Dunkirk and the evacuation scenes.

Spain's infamous dictator, General Franco, initially refused to give permission for us to use his Heinkel squadron, and I remember the subject of Gibraltar was mentioned and (much like it still is today) was politically very sensitive. (In fact, the following year Franco ordered the frontier crossing closed and it remained so for thirteen years.) After much persuasion on our part, with paperwork and written assurances crossing back and forth, permission to borrow the thirty-two planes was finally secured. I dread to think what we'd have done had it not been agreed.

The Spanish painters seemed to enjoy decorating their nation's fighter aircraft in German colours, but we were asked to hold back on adding the black crosses and swastikas until the last minute, as the planes were still in active use and the idea of them flying over southern Spain resplendent in German markings wasn't something the authorities were very keen on!

Tony Rimmington, who I'd first met on *Lawrence of Arabia*, joined the production as the other assistant art director and he specialised in the planes' arms and armour, initially setting about making dummy 50kg bombs which had to be dropped in flight. We tried it out with a run out over the sea, with the newly restored release mechanism all oiled and checked. Mindful of the situation with Gibraltar, I suggested to Tony that 'loading Spanish planes with bombs to fly out near British territory is probably a Tower of London offence'!

'Blimey, you could be right,' he said, but, in the name of film-making we threw all caution to the wind and carried on bravely.

The very first day of filming was actually a scene of Goering alighting from his train at Iruzan, up in the hills around San Sebastian, and we invited three of the original German fighter aces to join us on set – Adolf Galland, Colonel Hans Brustellin and Major Franz Frodl. Unfortunately our director, Guy Hamilton, in stepping from the raised platform onto the metal step of Goering's carriage, slipped and fell down between the train and platform badly grazing both his shins. However, not to be outdone by the 'enemy' he looked up and said, 'things can only get better'!

I then travelled to near San Sebastian, for the erection of the Cap Gris-Nez obelisk – where Goering looks out at the white cliffs of Dover – but to my horror, in the sixteen weeks since we'd been there to select the location, a building company had moved in, flattened the entire area and started putting up

▲▲ Tony Oliver is backing up the Hor staff car with director Guy Hamilton and cinematographer Freddie Young looking on.

▲ Goering (played by Hein Riess) at Cap Gris.

▲ Harbour scenes of the build-up to Operation Sea Lion, shot at Fuenterrabia in the north of Spain.

houses! I knew before I phoned the production office what their answer would be, and I was right: 'Well, find another similar location.'

Overcoming problems is something we face on a daily basis in the film business, and sometimes if I'm honest, I thrive on it. I did find another site for my 55ft tall monument, and just as I sat back feeling quite pleased with myself, I heard news of another problem – the Spanish Air Ministry wanted their/ our entire Heinkel fleet to take part in a NATO exercise over the Atlantic before performing a flypast for all the NATO big cheeses ... and, yes, that meant all aircraft had to revert to Spanish markings for two days (and back to German ones afterwards)! Apart from the cost and my rising blood pressure, the potential disruption to our filming schedule was

colossal. I really did wonder if Guy Hamilton had spoken too soon.

Needless to say, protests were made at the highest levels and, somehow, someway, it was agreed that the Heinkels would take part in the exercise, but in their Luftwaffe colours. I often wondered what the NATO chiefs thought of their flypast, though.

Along with the German pilots, I was incredibly lucky to meet some of the real life heroes from the Allied side: Lord Dowding (Air Chief Marshall), Group Captain Douglas Bader, Wing Commander Bob Stanford Tuck and Squadron Leader Ginger Lacey. Sadly, Lord Dowding was then confined to a wheelchair, and Douglas Bader was none-too-agile either, but with the assistance of Ginger Lacey he couldn't wait to climb up and sit in a Spitfire once more.

With location work in Spain completed we returned to England, and I moved across to Duxford Airfield where the majority of other sequences were being filmed. I felt rather pleased that my journey from home to Duxford, in my Triumph Spitfire, took less time than driving from home to Pinewood, so I had the luxury of not having to leave home until 6.30 a.m., taking breakfast in the hangar and then casually walking over to report for duty just as my London-based colleagues came tearing through the gates.

One air-raid sequence required the complete destruction of a hangar at Duxford – long before it was converted into the country extension of the Imperial War Museum (IWM) that it is today – and they willingly agreed we could do it for real. The general feeling was that the site would probably be all sold off for housing development or, as another rumour had it, an open prison. But, thanks to the IWM being allowed to store some planes and tanks there, which they didn't have room for in London, the idea of it becoming a museum fast gained support from all quarters and

I'm delighted to say I still visit the place today to see one of the best collections of aircraft and vehicles in the whole of Europe.

Of course, many planes were destroyed during the hangar bombing scenes, and so after taking moulds

▲▲ One of thirty-two Heinkel bombers used in the film.

▲ A scene on the outskirts of Tablada Airfield, home of the Spanish Air Force.

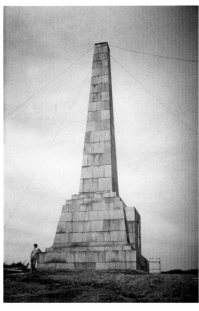

⌃ The Cap Gris set, with the obelisk under construction.

of Spits and Hurricanes, scores of disposable fibre-glass ones poured out of the workshops at Pinewood and were sent down to the airfield. It's amazing to think that only a few of the planes you see on the fields in the film were actually real.

When it came to filming the London Blitz scenes, Jack Maxstead (my boss) and I had to find rows of terraced houses that were due for demolition as part of the 'slum clearance programme of the Greater London Council (GLC)' around the Camberwell Road area. We suggested pulling down four houses in the centre of a row, and leaving the bricks piled around to look, literally, like a bomb had hit. The GLC demolition team were all in agreement, but I was curious as to how they'd be able to pull four houses down without explosives (which they weren't allowed to use).

'Explosives?' they asked, surprisingly, before showing me a thick hawser cable which they fed through the front door of one house, down the hallway and into the kitchen, before pulling it through

▲ Two of the lead cast, Susannah York and Christopher Plummer.

the garden and reversing the route into the next door kitchen, hallway and through the front door ... and so on through the four houses. Both ends of the cable were then connected to a heavy Caterpillar tractor and, with one swift tug, the old cement holding the bricks in place crumbled and reduced everything to a pile of rubble.

I ventured inside most of the other houses that were due for demolition and couldn't help but think about all the births, deaths and lives of the people that had occurred in each and to imagine how the houses had all survived the worst of the real Blitz ... until now. But at least the families who were evicted were relocated to the luxury flats that eventually replaced them. A slight irony was that the production actually paid the GLC for allowing us to pull down some of the slums that they were demolishing anyway.

We added a few little flourishes of our own with the odd old, iron bedstead and bits of furniture – icing on the cake you might say.

Our unit base during these scenes was actually the local pub, which proved quite handy when it started to rain in the middle of the night. Lord Snowdon joined us, as he was on board to take photographs of the Blitz scenes, but as the clock ticked past closing time the landlord could only give his beer away, for fear of losing his licence if he charged us. That was probably just as well, as can you imagine the headlines: 'Queen's brother-in-law in after-hours drinking party scandal in the East End'!

We did actually give the publican a few quid to donate to a charity of his choice in thanks for serving us die-hards. ❏

8 *A Touch of Class* (1973)

FILM CREDITS

A Touch of Class
Director: Melvin Frank
Stars: George Segal,
Glenda Jackson

▼ The famous (or infamous!) football team with our leading lady Glenda Jackson, who was to present the 'cup'. Unfortunately, the whole match ended in farce.

Our studio on this film was anything but classy – it was a converted biscuit factory overlooking the Grand Union Canal in Kensal Road, London. It would be fair to say that the largest area available within was an old store room, with a support column dead centre, and all the larger sets had to incorporate this column in some way or other.

I was sent ahead to Spain to prepare locations there, and when I finally arrived at the hotel overlooking the seafront in Guadalmina, it was obvious from the vast piles of sand, rubble and building supplies surrounding it that it was a brand new building. It turned out I was its first guest on its first day, and all the staff lined up to greet me.

I unpacked and left to do some measuring at the Golf Hotel, which was to be one of our locations, and when I returned to my abode I was told I couldn't use

the elevator to my third floor room, as they had begun to fill the swimming pool on the roof and water was pouring down the lift shaft!

As they'd opened the restaurant up just for me I felt obliged to eat there, and had three waiters looking after me, so I couldn't fault the service, but I was so glad when the Spanish crew arrived the next day to take the pressure off me having to keep the staff and chef occupied.

During my further location scouting I met up with 'Lord John' who owned a string of men's clothes shops in London, and he asked if I would like to see a deserted village up in the hills. It sounded like the perfect setting, so I agreed to meet him and his wife on the Sunday morning to head over there. We drove up dirt tracks, over the foothills of the Serrania De Ronda for about an hour and, sure enough, there it was.

I ventured into the church where, eerily, the numbers of the last hymns sung at the last service were still displayed. Next, I found the bar with a few intact glasses on the counter and dust everywhere. The village had been deserted for a few years, and I half expected tumbleweed to blow down the main street. Quite why the place had been abandoned was never made clear – perhaps everyone had left in search of work nearer the coast?

John knew of the place because his grandmother once owned a house nearby, which was now all boarded up, and had said that one day it would be his. We pulled the boards from the front door, climbed a staircase to the first floor, and entered the dining room. It was absolutely covered with pigeon droppings! The local birds had obviously been using it as

their nesting area and, perhaps under their weight, the chandelier had crashed down onto the long dining table below, and its baubles were all over the floor. Suddenly, the silence was broken by footsteps coming up the stairs – it turned out to be a local farmer, and he was the caretaker of the property. Seeing him brandishing a shotgun wasn't something I felt terribly happy about, so I made good my exit whilst John explained in his best Spanish who he was, and why he was there.

Freddie Cooper, our camera operator, checks a shot with Glenda Jackson whilst shooting the Mijas market scenes.

▲ Glenda Jackson with George Segal.

Later, with our location shoot in the can, our associate producer Peter Beale had the idea of throwing a BBQ on the beach to thank our Spanish crew, and that idea developed into a friendly game of football beforehand. I was never a footballer, and didn't appreciate being shouted at and being told I was offside; though if you fell over, I discovered, two young girls in hot pants ran out with cool sponges soaked in Spanish white wine to help revive you! Unfortunately, it all ended badly when our electricians went for the Spanish referee and chased him off the pitch. Our star, Glenda Jackson, threw down the winner's cup in disgust, and so unfortunately the chef on the beach, cooking the roast pig, had very few takers. The gallons of ice cream we had lined up for pudding were taken to the local village for the children.

Back in London, Vickie's (Glenda Jackson) flat was set in Soho, just off Shaftesbury Avenue, and with all

the necessary permissions in hand we started filming one Sunday. We hadn't banked on the increasing swell of the watching crowd, and the local bobby on the beat closed us down for obstruction. He wasn't interested in what pieces of paperwork we had! With only two or three of the scenes filmed, we had no option but to go back to base. There was no question of us returning the following Sunday, as it would have proved too expensive, and so we set up a whole load of Chinese signs along one side of Kensal Road, and set the camera angles such that we followed Glenda looking up at the signage. I defy anyone to watch the film and say we weren't in Soho. ❏

9 *The Mackintosh Man* (1973)

After we finished working on *A Touch of Class*, Terry Marsh was asked by Warner Bros to design a cold war spy thriller, which John Huston was hired to direct. It was set to star Paul Newman and James Mason – arguably two of Hollywood's biggest names of the period – and was going to be shot in Ireland, London and Malta, along with studio work at Pinewood.

Terry brought me on board as art director, and asked me to handle the initial studio work, with the plan being for me to fly out to Malta afterwards to find further locations whilst the unit were in Ireland shooting.

At the airport, before taking my plane to Malta, I was asked to meet Paul Newman's brother, Arthur. He was the advance party flying in from Ireland, and he was to accompany me. Arthur had been engaged as 'assistant to the producer', John Foreman, and in fact he worked on a lot of Paul's films in one capacity or another. He could have easily passed as Paul's twin, and he would have done perfectly had he not sported a totally shaven head (very unusual at that time) which, in fact, made him look more like Yul Brynner's brother from the eyes up.

FILM CREDITS

The Mackintosh Man
Director: John Huston
Stars: Paul Newman

◀ Cameraman Doug Milsome with a 'hidden' camera, filming Paul Newman in Leather Lane market.

➤ Paul Newman walking through the market.

In chatting on board the plane, I innocently told Arthur that one of our top location managers was coming out a few days after us, to help tie everything up, little realising that Arthur was fully expecting to be in charge of the whole location. He was quite furious and said he'd be having words with his brother to order a change of plan. I felt terribly guilty – not only had I upset our star's brother, I'd also put the kibosh on a job for a mate of mine, who I had worked with many times previously! But then again, at least I saved him the embarrassment of flying out to Malta only to be discharged.

First on our list of requirements was to find a sandy beach. It sounds easy, until you realise that there aren't any natural beaches on the island, nor on the neighbouring island of Gozo. The few possible spots which I identified as possible candidates (with the help of a bit of extra imported sand) from my boat journey around the island turned out to be totally inaccessible by land – which meant we couldn't get any of the travelling circus of trucks, generators and caravans anywhere near.

I placed a call to the unit back in Ireland to tell them that the 'sandy beach' really wasn't going to happen, and asked for John Huston's thoughts on an alternative. Word came back that he'd settle for a nice villa with a pool. As luck would have it, I'd spotted a villa the previous day as I was climbing a hill away from Marsaxlokk harbour – its blue pool stood out like a glittering sapphire in the barren valley. My driver was able to find his way down to the house, picking his way through a potholed track and, with some trepidation about inflicting an entire film crew on this peaceful, tranquil home, I knocked on the door.

The English gentleman who opened it looked slightly familiar, but in all my sputtering and babble about who I was and why I was there I didn't really think about who he might be. As he was so welcoming in inviting me in and introducing me to his wife, I wanted to cut straight to the chase and state our requirements and not waste his time. As he listened intently to my proposition, his wife went off to make some coffee, and as I turned around from the sofa to reply to her 'do you take sugar?' I noticed a framed photograph of the very same gentleman in full football kit on the sideboard. It was at that moment the penny dropped – I was talking to Sir Stanley Matthews, probably the greatest ever British footballer! He'd retired and spent a lot of time here at his holiday home where, amongst other things, he coached the local football team.

Although we didn't want to film inside the house, only around the pool, Sir Stanley didn't seem terribly keen, saying he'd once been warned by producer-director team Betty Box and Ralph Thomas to 'never let film companies near your property'. I knew I'd have to work hard to convince him, and also knew money probably wouldn't be the motivating factor in this instance, and so, in thinking about that heavily potholed road we drove down and how it would need to be repaired to take the heavy generator, I sug-

◄ Little did I know that the house I was trying to secure for filming belonged to Sir Stanley Matthews!

gested we'd happily repair the 450ft long track with a new road surface. Little did I realise he'd been trying for two years to get the local council to do just that, so my offer was manna from heaven as far as he was concerned.

The next morning, I arranged with the local Maltese Government official to send a road grader and heavy steamroller to start the works – when you're spending a lot of money in a country desperate for dollar investment, you can get things moving very quickly! Of course, Sir Stanley was mightily impressed – not only was I true to my word, but I worked fast too.

When Huston arrived, he seemed pleased with the location but said he wanted to rewrite the script to accommodate it better. Within minutes it was typed and handed out to the actors, and just a few minutes later was 'in the can'. The quickest turnaround time I ever witnessed, from new script pages to being filmed.

⌃ Between takes John Huston liked to play backgammon with his star.

With location shooting underway, as with any big film it was customary to hold evening meetings where we'd discuss any potential problems that might arise the following week. Indeed, at one such gathering the subject of the 'night location of the church exterior' was raised. The church in question – as per the script – was positioned very close to the harbour edge, and lighting the whole harbour behind would certainly prove an enormous and difficult job, so in effect we'd really just see the church in the foreground with only darkness beyond. John Huston asked, 'How will we know the church is near the harbour?'

The wise men who were gathered around the table scratched their heads whilst trying to think of a way around the issue, so I dared to raise my hand and suggested we park a few fishing boats alongside the church wall. To say the dagger-looks I received from the rest of the assembled were hostile would be an understatement, but when I saw the warm Irish smile

across Huston's face I knew I'd found the simple and obvious solution.

On the night itself, I lined up all the fishing boats along the church exterior, allowing sufficient gaps for Paul Newman to duck and dive between them, in order that he could rescue the damsel in distress from the bad guy (James Mason) inside. I thought it all looked very atmospheric and interesting – well, as far as my knowledge of set-ups go at least.

Just then it started to rain, a very fine, steady rain which you think isn't wetting you, and it looked absolutely perfect. So Colin Brewer, the first assistant director, placed the call through to Huston's hotel to say we were ready for him. 'Send Alan to see me,' Huston said.

I quickly jumped in a car and was driven to his hotel on the other side of the island, where his long-time assistant Gladys Hill showed me into his suite. John was sitting up in bed, wearing silk pyjamas which had his initials emblazoned on a breast pocket, and he was surrounded by the previous day's British newspapers. 'My boy,' he said, 'this was your idea; just go back and tell Paul I'm letting you direct him through the scene, talk it over with him – it's easy, just a bit of action and a little dialogue. Once you're happy the crew can wrap.'

'Me, happy?! What about Paul?' I asked myself. I returned to the unit, stepped out of the car and, seeing I was alone, Colin, along with the lighting cameraman Ossie Morris, asked, 'What's happening? What did John want to see you for?'

I knew I'd likely ruffle a lot of feathers, so very calmly and assuredly said, 'He asked me to direct Paul in this scene, and won't be coming out here tonight.' My answer was met by much derision, with Colin Brewer saying, 'Be it on your head then'. That was hardly the encouragement I'd hoped to hear as I was about to set sail into my first adventure of directing. I knocked on Paul's trailer, explained what had happened and told

'OK Paul, if you'd like that's fine by me. First positions everyone'.

Colin Brewer, somewhat perplexed as to how I'd just effortlessly taken over from John Huston without a word of concern from the star, asked what I'd discussed with Paul in the trailer, to which I replied, 'a director never reveals what he says to his actors'.

Off we went again … and again … but after three takes, with the crew looking stony-faced at me and getting wetter by the minute, and with Paul having great fun with the scene behaving as though we were the oldest of buddies, I told Paul I couldn't keep a straight face any longer. We called a wrap, and that marked the end of my directorial career – but boy, I can imagine what any director would give to say they'd worked with Paul Newman!

At Pinewood we'd been told that an American stunt man was coming over to perform the motorbike prison escape sequence, which would see him jump with his bike over 24ft high walls. I said to Stuart Craig, the film's other art director, 'that's just impossible'.

'I know that, you know that, but this guy says he'll do it,' Stuart replied.

Anyhow, the stuntman arrived in London with his girlfriend, and enjoyed great hospitality at the Dorchester Hotel from where, every day, he was chauffeured out to the studio to practise. Mind you, jumping off the 4ft ramp he had asked us to set up on the backlot didn't quite seem enough 'training' to me, considering the actual jump in the film was six times that height. However, our stuntman remained confident all was in hand. That is, until a few days before the shoot date when he arrived at the studio with his leg in plaster; saying that unfortunately he now couldn't perform the jump. How he broke his leg I never knew, but he and his girlfriend packed up their hotel room and headed back to the US after a rather

him I was not at all a popular member of the crew that evening, so the best thing would be to get it in one and wrap. 'No,' said Paul, 'I think we should milk it a bit and drive them mad'.

A few minutes later, we both walked on to the set and Paul walked around to pace out his route. With his subsequent thumbs-up the cameraman called 'speed' and I shouted 'Action!' Paul did it exactly as planned, the camera panned with him throughout without any problems, so I called, 'Cut!'

'Perfect Paul!' I exclaimed.

'No, I think we should go again, Alan,' he said, 'that is, if you don't mind?'

˄ John Huston and Paul Newman discussing a scene.

nice London sojourn, and another brave performer was dispatched to meet us.

The replacement looked at the storyboards, queried the height of the wall and said, 'that's impossible!'

Of course, we now had the problem of Paul's character being in prison with no scripted way of getting him out and moving the story along, and word went around the studio that 'if anyone has any ideas, to submit them to John Huston'. Being a helpful sort of chap, I thought of one: a stolen crane parks up by the prison wall, smoke grenades are thrown over and into the exercise yard, and amid the in-fighting and confusion, our hero jumps onto a scramble net which has been lowered into the yard by the crane. Once over, they race away on two motorbikes. Huston liked my offering, and rewarded me with two weeks' extra salary for getting the film out of a dead end.

Back at Pinewood, every Friday the custom was for the art department (and others) to go to the local pub for lunch. Terry Marsh and I settled at a table in the public bar, and a few minutes later John Huston and Paul Newman arrived and sat down at a table near the far end of the bar – raising many local eyebrows as they did so. We acknowledged them with a friendly smile and continued our lunch, but I couldn't help noticing that whilst he was chatting with Paul, John kept pointing towards me. He eventually called Terry over for a word, and when he returned to our table grinning widely, Terry wouldn't let me in on what they'd said to him. 'I'll tell you later' was all he'd say.

Driving back to the studio, Terry revealed that John wanted me to play a role in the film and wanted to see me about it that afternoon. I nearly swerved off the road and into a ditch. As soon as I got back into the office, I picked up a copy of the script and hurriedly looked through the pages we had left to shoot, and then broke out in a cold sweat. The part was in the prison laundry with Paul and had about six pages of dialogue – oh, and the character smoked, which I had never done.

I went over to John's office and apologised, saying, 'it just isn't for me'. I'd never had any ambitions to direct, let alone act, and here was John Huston suggesting me for both roles on this film! But John has a habit of always getting what he wants and, charming as ever, he smiled and said he would 'look after' me and I should give it my best shot.

After two sleepless nights worrying how I might get out of it, and knowing nothing I could say to John would influence him against me, I came up with an idea. I knew there were hundreds of out-of-work actors who'd kill for the role playing opposite Paul Newman, so I went to see the casting director, Weston Drury Jnr, and pleaded with him to help me out and find one that fitted the description in the script. He, in turn, suggested John Bindon (a reformed gangster and jailbird) to John, and you might say it was perfect casting all round!

10 *A Bridge Too Far* (1975)

I started work on *A Bridge Too Far* shortly after finishing on a film with Gene Wilder called *The Adventure of Sherlock Holmes' Smarter Brother*, and happily we kept the same art department team together, under Terry Marsh's production design leadership.

The first recce to Holland took place on 13 October 1975. Terry, along with art director Stuart Craig, our construction manager Peter Dukelow and myself, went to look at a similar bridge to the one at Arnhem, in Deventer, because Arnhem Bridge itself was completely surrounded with modern buildings – a far cry from the wartime setting we were looking to recreate.

Deventer, only 35km from Arnhem, was ideal. This bridge over the River Ijssel was of similar design, that

FILM CREDITS

A Bridge Too Far
Director: Richard Attenborough
Stars: Sean Connery, Ryan O'Neal, Michael Caine, Dirk Bogarde

◄ The completed gliders lined up on the runway.

One of the sets we built (and then destroyed) next to the main bridge.

is to say, it was a 'coat hanger' type construction, although slightly shorter and not quite so wide – you might say it was a 90 per cent scale model of the Arnhem Bridge. The other advantage, around the ramp up to the bridge, was a huge car park on which we would be able to construct our five houses (see photos on p. 67). All of the houses were constructed to be partially destroyed during filming, with areas of polystyrene bricks set into the walls for F/X explosions, etc.

So, having measured up and photographed both bridges, we returned to our UK base – an empty High Street shop adjacent to Twickenham Film Studios. Who said film-making is glamorous?

The first job was to construct a model to show our director, Richard Attenborough, and with it, the proposed building program around the bridge. Half the houses were built for real so that we could shoot inside on all levels. We also included the block of modern flats into the model to show the camera angles that wouldn't work (see photo on p. 69). Knowing that the construction unit was shipping out to Holland immediately after the Christmas break, we tried to complete all the drawings of the buildings and the gliders so we could start building straight away in an empty factory just outside Deventer.

The journey over to the Hook of Holland was one of the worst crossings I've ever experienced. It was so rough that the bow of the ferry was damaged in docking. The Dutch people were so welcoming, and on our first Sunday there we were all invited to the local English Speaking Society's New Year party. The clubhouse was decorated with table centrepieces made of fir tree branches and lots of lit candles.

During the evening, my young son (I had all my family with me) noticed that the candles had burned down to their bases in the next room and set the

▲ The art department model created to show director Richard Attenborough what we planned to build either side of the bridge.

◄ A composite shot of the finished set, taken with my little pocket camera from the roof of a building opposite.

dried fir tree pieces alight. In trying to instil good manners, namely that he – like other children – should be seen and not heard, I initially refused to listen to him as I was preoccupied talking to the local mayor, but thankfully he kept pulling my sleeve saying 'Dad, Dad' and a much bigger fire was averted.

We had started building the six 'Horsa gliders' from drawings that Tony Rimmington had done prior to leaving the UK, and to keep the price down we opened up the space between the ply ribs and wing formers, knowing ours only had to be towed down the runway and not endure the stress of flight. This gave us a problem. On damp mornings the 88ft wingspan had a droop each end! So, a long 'H' iron girder was

inserted into the top of each glider to keep the wings straight. It gave us real respect for the construction of the original flying plywood monsters, only 7ft shorter than a C-47 (Dakota) wingspan.

My office was the closest to the factory entrance, and on one occasion a guy looking remarkably like Clint Eastwood came in saying he was a KLM pilot flying jumbo jets. He said he would like to volunteer to fly one of our Dakota fleet at Deelen Airfield.

The rumour was, if you wanted to obtain a lot of RAF aircraft then ex-Group Captain Hamish Mahaddie was the man to track them down for you. Hamish was the man responsible for rounding up all the aircraft we used on *Battle of Britain*, and prior to that, arranging all the Lancasters for the 1954 film

▼ American fighters were ordered up to drop purple smoke in scenes of the Irish guards trying to get through to Arnhem.

The Dam Busters. He procured eleven Dakotas – two ex-Portuguese Air Force; two from Djibouti Airways; four Finnish Air Force Dakotas and three Danish Dakotas. Naturally, much work was done to each aircraft to meet both the Civil Aviation Authority and the Federal Aviation Administration safety licences required to carry passengers.

Parachute hook-up wires had to be fitted back into each plane, as in wartime, and the British Parachute Regiment were made available to us via a Ministry of Defence exercise, code named 'New Market / Gulls Wing'. All the paras, having just returned from Berlin, were whisked off to the Airborne Museum at Aldershot to carry out the aircraft familiarisation

training for jumping from a Dakota. Wing Commander Mike Jenkins of HQ 38 Group was to be in charge of all the training and planning for the team that performed all the parachute drops on the film.

Many mischievous stories were put about in Aldershot about how, when you jump from a Dakota, the chances are that you would hit the tail. However, apart from one parachutist who, at the last minute, refused to jump, all of our five mass jumps (of approximately 350 men) went off well. Sadly, the cost of a jump refusal for that fellow was a court martial sentence of eighty-five days' detention!

People ask me how we got the shots from a glider pilot's point of view, looking down the tow rope to a Dakota, if none of our Horsa gliders flew. Without all the benefits of current digital additions, we simply got a glider from the London Gliding Club at Dunstable to be towed aloft with the addition of a cameraman alongside the pilot.

Towards the end of filming, we were asked to paint out all the roundels of the RAF Dakotas and replace them with American 'Stars and Bars' markings. Unfortunately, we had sent all our painters back to the UK so, together with the second unit standby painter, the art department spent the day repainting all the markings on a number of Dakotas.

It was said at the time that the Dakotas were painted in the wrong colour. Not wanting to make the same mistake as on *Lawrence of Arabia*, where the aeroplanes in the *correct* camouflage disappeared (as they should) in all the air-to-ground shots, we decided that instead of using the standard green and brown camouflage scheme, we would use the equally correct European olive drab scheme. The colour was given to me down at Aldershot and was checked against the Tamiya model paint supplies (the Japanese are sticklers for accuracy with all their paints). Once I was satisfied

▲ The set under construction.

➤ Here I am, putting the finishing touches to the bridge that was fitted into the model.

▲ Partially built gliders in our workshop in Deventer.

➤ A German column coming over Nijmegen Bridge during our short permitted closure, early on a Sunday morning.

that the two matched, the chosen colour was mixed up in sufficient quantities to paint eleven Dakotas. When all the planes were finished and lined up on the runway, the technical advisor – without having the advantage of the research I had done – asked Richard Attenborough why they were painted in desert camouflage. I was naturally called to the set to explain, though it didn't cut much ice up against the 30-year-old memory of this veteran colonel who only remembered the RAF Dakotas in the green and brown markings.

Due to the schedule requirements of the twelve main actors, we were asked to prepare the gliders in their crashed state *before* they were to be shot in parked formations, prior to being towed along the runway for the boarding scenes. This is the somewhat crazy side of film-making!

The closure of the Nijmegen Bridge for the scenes where Robert Redford, playing the com-

manding officer of 3rd Battalion 504 PIR (82nd Airborne), crosses the river and takes the bridge, was a mammoth undertaking for the production department. Nijmegen Bridge, one of the biggest in Europe, would only give the film company clearance for an hour's work, from 8 a.m. to 9 a.m. on a Sunday morning. This window of opportunity covered not only vehicular traffic, but also all the river traffic that would be going under the bridge. Therefore, you can imagine how the pre-planning of this one hour was one of the most intensive on the whole film.

Even so, one lone man, totally unaware of what was going on, put out from the shore close to the bridge

◄ 'Grabner's Charge'.
Recreating the German attack
on the bridge, with the crew
looking on.

▲ The famous folding boats, shown here going across the Grave Bridge on their way to Nijmegen.

➤ Joseph E. Levine, our producer, showing off his new walking-stick handle against the background of Arnhem Bridge.

➤➤ Deventer Bridge, showing the similarity to Arnhem Bridge.

in a small boat. He must have suddenly realised that there was nothing moving on the bridge or the river as he made his way out to the middle. Before he could even scratch his head, two police launches, blue lights flashing, raced towards him and he stood up in his little boat with his hands up. Once he had been 'escorted' off the set, 'Action!' boomed out again from loud speakers situated at each camera position.

I researched the construction of the British Army's standard collapsible canvas boats down at the Royal Marines' Museum in Southsea, and was amazed that they could carry ten men on the water and could, in turn, be carried by four men, as they weighed only 150kg (330lb). They looked, it must be said, very flimsy. They had a plywood base with two boat-shaped outer ply rings and, once the canvas was pulled up to its full extent, four very small struts were clipped into place to maintain the tension of the stretched canvas. They were devised by Fred Goatley and were duly named after him. Over 1,000 of these 'Goatley boats' were ordered for the commandos during the war.

With safety a priority, and carrying many extras (let alone famous actors), we employed the very best boat builders, and as such, Mike Turk Film Services based in Richmond took on the job. They had built boats for films for many years – from galleons to royal barges – and ours were built to exacting standards; though I can't help thinking that if 'Health & Safety' were around then, sending Robert Redford and about eighty fully kitted-out soldiers into a fast-flowing, wide river would have caused a few heated discussions. Of course, we had trained divers in each boat in case of mishaps, but thankfully, apart from getting soaked to the skin, no harm came to any of the boats' occupants.

◄ Recreating the big parachute drop.

◄◄ My young son on one of the tanks. He's now an art director himself and, at the time of writing, is working on *Stars Wars VII*.

▼ A derelict house was partly rebuilt to represent the Hartenstein Hotel set.

➤ Yours truly, with Ex-Lieutenant Colonel Giles Vandeleur, who led the Irish Guards in the dash to Arnhem (he was played by Michael Caine in the film). The other officer was in charge of the tank training ground on which we were filming.

▼ Gene Hackman, Ryan O'Neal, Michael Caine, James Fox and Dirk Bogarde – just a few of the all-star cast!

The budget was said to be around $26 million which, at that time, was a massive amount, but our canny producer Joseph E. Levine – on the back of the all-star cast, including Sean Connery, Laurence Olivier, Michael Caine, Gene Hackman and Anthony Hopkins, to name but a few – had pre-sold the distribution rights around the world and was in profit before the cameras started turning! ❏

◄ A candid snap of our director, Richard Attenborough, with director of photography, Geoffrey Unsworth.

◄ The first house under construction.

▼ Stuart Craig, who later went on to design the Harry Potter films, standing on the bridge.

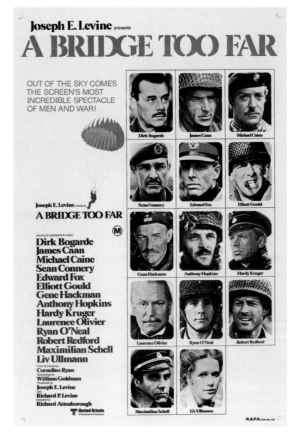

⌃ Stuart Craig and Terry
Marsh working on the art
department model prior to
shipping it out to Holland.

➤ Robert Redford arriving
on set for the first time.

⌃ The main building, almost complete.

11 *Hanover Street* (1977)

Hanover Street is set in war-torn London in 1943, where a courageous American bomber pilot (Harrison Ford) meets a British nurse (Lesley-Anne Down) during a massive air raid and they fall instantly in love, despite the fact she is married to a Secret Intelligence officer (Christopher Plummer). It's not long before the pilot has to drop the Secret Intelligence officer behind enemy lines – no prizes for guessing how these two men in her life finish up together on this secret mission.

My favourite period in reproducing sets and vehicles for films is that of the Second World War. Phillip Harrison, the production designer, sent me off to London to select period shop fronts that he could use to line each side of the street we were going to build. He also wanted to include one of those iconic plum-coloured tiled underground stations that were all over London. At the end of the street I was to reproduce the Hanover Square church, but reduce it in size without making it look too small against double-decker buses

FILM CREDITS

Hanover Street
Director: Peter Hyams
Stars: Harrison Ford, Lesley-Anne Down, Christopher Plummer

◀ The construction of our main street set, with completed church tower.

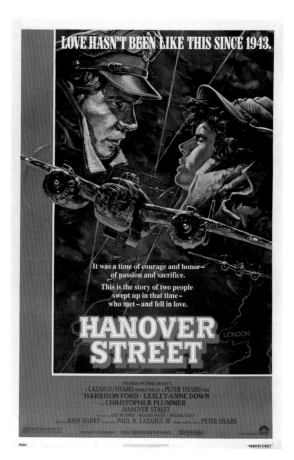

∧ The first establishing shot really brings the set to life.

driving by. The church had a Christopher Wren-style portico so, having hit on a size, I drew up the front elevation and then made a card model to show to Phillip for his approval. I even made a cardboard bus to prove we had the right size.

Work started through the bad winter of 1977/78. The night frosts played havoc with all the painting we had done during the day, since a lot of our paints were water-based, and each morning we could see vast areas that had not had a chance to dry out before the frost had ruined it.

The five B-25 bombers were assembled out at Bovingdon Airfield and, although it was only a few miles from my house, I sadly had little to do with that location as I was too busy with the street. We ended up with nearly 100 drawings in order for the

◄ My selfie, though I didn't get the whole church in!

▲ Harrison Ford poses on our set.

carpenters and plasterers to build that set. During the war, the airfield was home to the USAAF 92nd Bomb Group which flew B-17s and, as it was one of the closest American airfields to London, it was said that General Eisenhower kept his personal B-17 there.

I was asked by Jeff Hawke (our aircraft supplier) if I wanted to fly out to the States with him and bring back another B-25. Having seen the video he made of the return trip I was pleased I did not get sucked into the idea. At one point he tells his crew, whilst banging an oil gauge, 'either it is a faulty gauge or we best prepare ourselves to ditch into the Atlantic – prepare the dinghies just in case'! Luckily it was a faulty gauge, but I was pleased I did not have to with-stand that sort of startling information, especially as I would have only packed three lots of underwear for the three day trip!

The painting, especially of exteriors, had to be totally realistic. I had noticed that the weather side on all the Purbeck white stonework buildings around London is washed white, while the other side is stained brown with all the London air pollution over many years. I told the painter to ensure the eight columns of the porticoed church were painted this way but he wouldn't believe me, so I managed to get a car to take him to the church from the production office to see for himself.

Westminster Council loaned us one of their 1930s decorative lamp posts from which to take moulds, and we managed to reproduce at least five in fibreglass for the set. We strengthened them with a steel scaffold pole down the centre, only to find out that on windy days they waved around a bit, so the construction boys cut a hole at the top and poured concrete in until it set to fill the whole casting. Another problem solved!

One shot required the collapse of a three storey building into the street over a double-decker bus. The

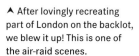 After lovingly recreating part of London on the backlot, we blew it up! This is one of the air-raid scenes.

➤ Lesley-Anne Down, with a young Patsy Kensit playing her daughter.

➤➤ Publicity shot of Harrison Ford and Lesley-Anne Down.

special effects guys rigged a hydraulic frame that would push forward on both sides of the block and push the front wall over as a bomb exploded within the building. Naturally, to achieve the proper effect, this wall was constructed from real bricks and not plaster brick sheets. On 'Action!' the whole front of the block fell realistically into the street.

The local residents living close to the studio backlot were warned that some pretty loud explosions would be disturbing their night-time rest but, as it happened, the noise was not as bad as had been feared over the three nights' shooting. The local newspaper

⋏ Setting up for the big jump.

◂ We reproduced old wartime street posters to obscure modern parts of the buildings and street behind.

Stunt rider Eddie Kidd gets
into character.

(the *Borehamwood Post*) said that it would not be as problematic or as long as 'when MGM had two weeks of night filming with lots of explosions for *The Dirty Dozen* ten years previously'.

One of our main locations was at Woodstock, the closest town to Blenheim Palace. The Town Hall in the main square doubled for the Gestapo Headquarters, where our heroes had to get dressed up as a German SS officer and his driver.

It was also in this area that I went off to find a cutting, about 80ft wide, that could be incorporated into our motorcycle chase. Someone told me that a seldom-used part of the preserved East Somerset Railway had a 60ft-deep cutting, but they did not know how wide it was at the top. So, thinking initially that I might be on another wild goose chase, I was happily surprised to find it more than suitable. Not able to measure exactly the distance that the stunt motorbike would have to clear, our producer Harry Benn thought the photos I took warranted taking our stuntman down to Doulting in Somerset to see if it was viable.

Nicknamed 'Britain's Evel Knievel', Eddie Kidd was going to do the jump, and he had recently been entertaining the public with some big show leaps of 80ft. If he felt it was too much of a jump, I had plans to narrow the cutting by building the remains of an old bridge abutment either side. As we walked across the adjacent field, he asked if I could put down a wooden track covered in chicken wire, so he could get up to a good speed, then have an angled board at the end to give him the desired lift he would need to clear the cutting. He then took one look at the cutting and said 'No problem'.

We laid the track as required, though not knowing the angle he required I made the last ramped rostrum adjustable. The next day was the big shot. A lot of

press had come down from London to witness the jump, so I asked Eddie prior to the shot, 'what angle should I adjust the ramp to?' His reply was typical of this very brave cockney stunt guy: 'Christ knows, I just give myself the sign of the cross and open the throttle'. You can imagine that put a lot of pressure on me to get the ramp at the right angle.

I think I was nearly as nervous as Eddie as he strapped the dummy of Christopher Plummer onto his back and did a couple of run-ups across the field.

I'm pleased to say that, after roaring along the ¼ mile track, he hurled himself and the dummy into the air, hitting the ground at 90mph, before flinging the bike to one side to bring himself to a stop. Eddie had, in fact, managed 145ft – some 40ft further than the world long distance jump record that he had set the year before.

Sadly, he had an accident in 1996 that left him paralysed and with brain damage, but that did not stop him entering the London Marathon in 2011 which raised thousands of pounds for his chosen charities. ❏

ʌ 'Eddie the eagle', on the bike over the railway cutting.

< A lovely lobby card shot of the motorcycle chase, just prior to a record-breaking jump.

12 *The Empire Strikes Back* (1978)

FILM CREDITS

Star Wars: The Empire Strikes Back
Director: Irvin Kershner
Stars: Mark Hamill, Harrison Ford, Carrie Fisher

Received Academy Award nomination

▼ Finse Station and Hotel, which was our base for the location – before the snowstorm and after.

When I worked on *2001* at MGM Studios, Borehamwood, I became good friends with John Barry who was then resident art director to Elliot Scott, MGM's head of design. In 1976, John approached me to join him on a sci-fi film called *Star Wars*, but I had just promised my services to *A Bridge Too Far* and had to decline the opportunity.

All throughout working on Kubrick's *2001*, John loved visiting our offices to see the futuristic concepts we were working on. I remember one particular day when he came in, very excited, and told us that he had been offered his first film as designer – *Kelly's Heroes*. Being MGM staff for many years, John didn't know many art directors outside of the studio, so he sought advice from John Graysmark and myself. We immediately recommended both Les Dilley and Norman Reynolds. It was following his success on *Kelly's Heroes* that John was offered the chance to design *Star Wars*, and both Les and Norman stayed with him – it turned out to be the film for which they all won Oscars.

I felt a little guilty in turning down John's kind invitation, though I sincerely knew I'd made the right choice with *A Bridge Too Far* when I asked him what the story was. He replied, 'it's about two robots in the desert, fighting good against evil'. How could anyone guess that this would become one of the most successful films of all time!

Almost two years later, however, I was asked by Norman Reynolds to join him on the second Star Wars film, *The Empire Strikes Back*. I didn't need to be asked twice, and reported for duty at Elstree Studios in late 1977. Stanley Kubrick was there, halfway through filming *The Shining*, and most of the big stages were full with his sets, but we were reassured he'd be wrapped on his film long before we started building.

▲ Camp Sharman, the defence line prior to attack.

◄ A dressed crowd of Stormtroopers walking to Camp Sharman for lunch.

▲ Special effects take out a gun position!

➤ Checking out the crashed snowspeeder.

➤➤ My daughter with R2-D2.

However, with no stage really big enough to build an ice hangar set (to house the Millennium Falcon), a decision was made to build our own stage that would be large enough to film all the scenes with the giant spaceship.

As the weeks went by we were naturally impatient to start building the myriad of sets required for the script, but *The Shining* started running over schedule. On top of that, a big fire completely destroyed Stage 3, meaning that the available space at Elstree was now minimal to say the least. What's more, the construction of our 'Star Wars Stage' was running behind schedule, so meetings were hurriedly organised to try and juggle our stage requirements as the shoot date fast approached.

Bill Welch, our construction manager, was faced with the enormous task of building sets faster than ever and then, after we'd filmed on them, having to strike them quicker than ever before as well. Lots of weekend work and night gangs were the order of the day.

Many locations for the ice planet 'Hoth' were considered. The script called for a treeless area of snow, ice and mountains, though of course it had to be accessible for the crew of about seventy people and all the equipment and generators needed. It became

a really tough call. That is, until Finse (an area in the Ulvik municipality of Hordaland, Norway) was suggested by one of the Norwegian Fox Distribution people, as they often took a train up to the area in winter for cross-country skiing. Aside from the bonus of it being on a mainline railway station accessible from both Oslo and Bergen, it had a hotel, a frozen lake and – at a height of 6,000ft – even its own glacier!

The risk, in deepest winter, of a crew getting stuck in a 'white-out' – that is, in blizzard conditions and with no visibility – was made clear to the production, when our Norwegian construction manager recalled a night he was caught in one blizzard. Like every well-equipped Norwegian, he was able to stop and build himself an igloo. Once out of the blizzard he eventually fell asleep. The next morning he awoke to the smell of frying bacon, and in digging out of his snow-blown igloo, he discovered he was only 100ft from the rear door of the hotel kitchens! Taking heed, we decided that we'd build a couple of emergency huts for the two most distant locations and fully equip them with

◄◄ Location transport: my snowmobile, without which I wouldn't have been able to get around!

▲ On my first rest day, the local Norwegian crew and I enjoy a drink at Camp Kurtz.

◄ Our probot, on its track.

▲ A snowspeeder under construction in tented workshops near the hotel.

➤ A snowspeeder at Disneyland.

➤➤ Me with a full-size walker (the only one reproduced at full scale) in Disneyland, Florida.

food, water and heating … just in case. One hut was named 'Camp Kurtz', after Gary, our producer, and the other 'Camp Sharman' after Bruce, our production supervisor.

Back at the studio, there were an inordinate number of meetings called about the Finse location. In fact, I wondered how they could have so many gatherings to plan just one element of the shoot. On top of those, at least three separate trips were made out

there and on each trip the snow was getting deeper and deeper. I was pleased not to be caught up in all of it, as I felt it really was taking up so much of everyone's time, leaving little time to discuss anything else in the schedule. Besides, I knew my colleague Les Dilley was assigned as location art director, so I wouldn't have anything to do with that particular sequence. Les was due to fly on the Monday morning, on the first plane to Oslo, but at 4 p.m. the day before Norman Reynolds rang me to say Les was sick, and his doctor said he should not travel. I knew what was coming next – would I take his place as location art director?

Well, like a good soldier, I packed a suitcase and was at Heathrow Airport at 5.30 the following morning. Naturally I was a bit apprehensive to go to a

▲ Here, I am fitting Anthony Daniels into his suit as C-3PO.

location I knew so little about, and kicked myself for complaining that so much time had been given over to discussions in the last five weeks. I now felt a bit like a schoolboy who had missed all the lessons, but was going in for the exam anyway! Fortunately, I travelled out with Bill Welch who was able to fill me in on a lot of the pre-planning, as he'd attended all of the meetings and had been on the last recce.

Finse was 1,222m above sea level, and the only way to move around in deep snow was on skis or a snowmobile, and on the first day we were given a brand new snowmobile each. The Swedish company

➤ Me, looking very cold on set!

▲ My certificate of Oscar nomination for the movie.

'Activ' were supplying all our snow equipment, and a small backup service team to keep them all running. We were shown how to make a quick igloo to crawl into to keep out the wind if we were ever stranded out in the open! It went on to snow every day, and with the temperature sinking well below -20°C we were sure glad of the many layers of clothing that the production had issued us with.

I had a bedroom on the first floor of the hotel overlooking the station, and during my time there the snow eventually reached the bottom half of my window. Every morning before dawn the hotel staff would gamely clear the snow from the entrance so we could at least walk to our large tented workshops adjacent. We learnt that the snow never melts around the glacier location, even in summer, and because of

that it was selected way back in 1910 as the training ground for Captain Scott and his team prior to his ill-fated South Pole trek. We hoped our fate would be a bit more positive!

When the rest of the unit finally arrived it was in a severe blizzard and the Oslo–Bergen railway line was blocked by three separate avalanches. Snowplough trains, leaving from each end of the line, had a job to keep us from being completely cut off and isolated. Although, when the first day of shooting (5 March) arrived, the snow was so bad that the whole line had been impassable for two whole days. Fortunately we had all the equipment and crew we needed in place.

I had dressed our 'defence trench' for the first day's shooting. Travel there the next morning proved difficult, if near impossible, so having cannily noticed the mountainous snowdrift at the rear of the hotel we decided to film the first shots all within 30ft of our hotel comforts.

When the local crew said it was OK to venture out on our snowmobiles to the trench location later in the day, we found it had disappeared, along with all our expensive dressing. On advice from one of the locals we engaged the help of a gentleman who not only ran the local youth hostel, but also was called on to find people buried in avalanches. He arrived with a sort of water divining stick and told us where to start digging. Sure enough, all of our boxes, pipes etc., were there. From that day on, I always left exterior dressing to the very last minute, especially if it was in a trench.

With the weather dictating our outdoor shooting it was decided to bring Harrison Ford out a week early. We all thought the snowploughs would clear the railway tracks, but an area coming up from Oslo had a large snow-collapse onto the tracks, meaning the ploughs couldn't operate and it all had to be cleared by hand. Harrison was already en route by the time

effects man, had laid charges. As the cameras panned down slowly – counting down from five to one – they would blow the snow overhang to depict the landing. But the ever-changing and unpredictable weather continually frustrated us, and after waiting for hours for the cloud to lift we were forced to abandon the shoot as we were all frozen through. You can put up with the cold if you are accomplishing something, but trying to cope with extreme temperatures when you're just hanging around is quite unbearable.

The next morning dawned bright and clear, so off I went with the second unit to try again. All went well with the rehearsals, and at last we were ready to nail it. Peter McDonald (the second unit director) counted down, and on 'one' we expected to see the big over-hang of snow blow, but all we could hear was the noise of the wind. Peter was furious and screamed into his mobile radio, 'Allan Bryce come in', but nothing came back. Seeing Peter's anger building up I felt quite pleased I wasn't working the effects. I should never have thought that. The next name over the radio was mine: 'Get up there and see what the hell's happened to him!'

I began the climb up the 100ft mountain ridge and, waist deep in powder snow and gasping for air, I struggled to the top. Of course, being conscious of holding up the unit I overdid it. When I finally crawled around a rock at the top to see Allan, I was so breath-less I couldn't speak – all I could do was point at the battery on his radio, as I could see it had partly become disconnected. Allan clicked it back into place, and asked Peter why they were not shooting! To say the airwaves went blue would be an under-statement. It was made very apparent to Allan that the idea of working on this shot for so long, in a wind chill factor (even in the sunshine) of -32°C, was not one the crew relished nor wanted to repeat.

we received the news, but he could only get within 30 miles of us. As we'd planned to film scenes with him the next morning, a rescue plan was set in motion.

Our location manager took a bottle of Vodka to the driver of the snowplough engine and bribed him to go down the line as far as he could to pick up our leading actor, who'd agreed to walk part of the way. I was told that they all returned, very merry, about midnight. I guess the empty bottle was explained away as being 'medicinal'?

Once the weather improved I went up to the 'blue ice' area with the second unit to film the matte shot of the 'probot landing'. We set up the cameras facing a big overhang of snow, where Allan Bryce, the special

▲ In 2011, I attended the Elstree Studios Celebration day, as did these mean-looking Empire representatives.

With all the shots (finally) in the can, I left Finse with a forward party to travel on the first leg of our journey back to London. There were six of us, and we had an overnight stop in Bergen before heading to the airport the next morning. We all decided to find a good restaurant to celebrate leaving the snowy wastes of Finse far behind us. The restaurant in question came highly recommended, but on arriving I noticed it was full of men; there wasn't a single female dining. In fact Pamela Mann, our continuity girl, was the only woman there. Curious as to why, I asked the owner, who said that the last ever episode of *Dallas* was being shown that evening and all the women were at home watching it. The power of television strikes again, I thought.

John Barry, meanwhile, had left his other film project and was immediately offered a job by George Lucas and Gary Kurtz to come on board and direct the second unit on *Empire*. John, in turn, asked me to join him as his standby art director. He was so happy to reunite with many of his old team from the first *Star Wars*.

It was really nice to work with John again, even though the majority of what remained was blue screen work. Each morning at 7 a.m. we would all meet up in the preview theatre to view the previous day's rushes before our 8 a.m. start on the stage. On the second Friday into our schedule, John was not there. I was told he had the flu. In truth, he had collapsed in the production office and had been rushed to hospital. His high temperature of 105 degrees could not be reduced, and by 2 a.m. the next morning he had died. We later discovered he'd contracted meningitis from a trip to North Africa. It was all so sudden, and left us all stunned. To think that you can be around such a fun and talented man one day, and just twenty-four hours later that same person could die from such a terrible disease doesn't bear thinking about.

Ten days later, the whole production shut down after lunch so that we could all travel to John's funeral – highly unusual in the film business, let me tell you – which was held in a small church in Chiswick. It was attended by so many of his colleagues, including Stanley Kubrick and Stanley Donen, and this really reflected the high regard in which John was held.

Many months after *Empire* was completed, I took my children over to Disneyland in LA, and whilst there, Gary Kurtz's sister invited us for a tour of their Industrial Light & Magic studios to view all the models from *Star Wars*. It turned out to be the first Saturday in many months that no one was working, so we had the run of the place and I desperately hoped to find something from our work in England. Then I saw it! Tucked at the end of a shelf was my first prototype card model of the snow speeder which we'd sent over in the early days, together with the original design by our conceptual artist, Ralph McQuarrie.

I came away feeling so pleased that I had found a link from my work to theirs. ❏

13 *Victor Victoria* (1980)

This was a remake of a successful German film from 1933 called *Viktor Viktoria*.

Blake Edwards thought it would be a perfect film to bring his wife, Julie Andrews, into more serious roles as she was getting typecast after her Oscar winning performance on *Mary Poppins*.

The preparation for the film started in Los Angeles, prior to coming over to Pinewood Studios. The American designer Roger Maus (not pronounced 'mouse' but 'mawse', we were told), came over with three sketches by the Los Angeles art director, William Craig Smith. I was engaged, along with Tim Hutchinson, as a 'UK art director'.

Blake wanted to build everything. His thinking was that the British blue sky and green trees (well, it was summer) would not have fitted in to the warm sepia feel he sought for this 1930s film. Having watched the finished movie, he was right. It all blended into an almost theatre-lit production. It was actually refreshing to do everything in stages, away from external elements, and for once not have to worry about the (brief) British summer weather changing before our eyes.

FILM CREDITS

Victor Victoria
Director: Blake Edwards
Stars: Julie Andrews, James Garner

◀ Blake Edwards allows me to look through his viewfinder.

▲ This Parisian set was constructed on E-stage at Pinewood.

and the adjoining back-projection tunnel which enabled us to add another 100ft of street. I had the nice job of going over to Paris, armed with my camera and notebook, to find 1920s style shop fronts and cafés around the older areas of the city. I found most of the best ones around the Sacré Coeur area in old Montmartre. Having photographed them and taken overall dimensions, I returned with ample ideas to reconstruct them within our set.

Whilst I was in Montmartre, I also photographed the clever way they laid out the cobbled streets in fantails, which I wanted to replicate. I knew we would have to spread concrete to simulate cobblestones, especially as we had a rain sequence to cater for, so the photos helped me draw up a metal 'tamping mould' to push into the wet concrete to achieve the iconic pattern. It certainly is all 'smoke and mirrors' in this business.

We started construction on E-stage whilst Blake was still in Los Angeles, and word came from him that he wanted a stills photographer to record the building of the street twice a week. The production office obviously didn't want to pay a stills man a daily rate fee to come in for just an hour or two, so they asked me if I would volunteer for the task. I had hoped I might be

My first task was to make a model of the Parisian street set that was going to fill Pinewood's E-stage,

◄ We even recreated part of the Gare du Nord for the end sequence.

able to record the construction for my own interest, but now it was official!

I set up two camera positions from the studio floor that would cover all the best angles, and two more from the rafters, 40ft above the stage. Every two days I set up my tripod on the same spots and, on a set exposure because of the low light levels, took my snaps. Each roll of negative was printed up to 10in x 8in enlargements and parcelled up to give to Blake, showing him the progress. By the time the set was finished I had over 100 photos in three boxes. I took them over to Blake's office when he arrived at the studio, but by then his interest had waned, and he suggested I keep them. So, I still have one of the best records I know of a set being constructed.

It was about this time that the news came through that I had been nominated for an American Academy Award for the art direction on the second Star Wars film, *The Empire Strikes Back*. The next day, a bottle of champagne arrived on my desk with a card of congratulations from Blake and Julie. I was really moved by their kindness, so when I saw Blake on the set I naturally went up to thank him. Surprisingly he did not know what the hell I was talking about; Julie had arranged it but had never told him. Anyhow, my respect for Julie's talents and kindness is unswerving.

The interior café scenes, where Julie tries to get a free dinner by slipping a cockroach (that she had caught in her little attic room and hidden in a match-box) into her salad, were great fun to shoot. What

▲ Roger Maus with construction manager, Albert Blackshaw (on the right), then me, Tim Hutchinson and Ted Ambrose on the main set.

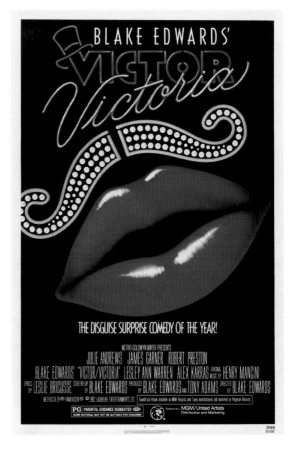

we did not know was that Julie was terrified of cockroaches, so Blake made sure a double was standing by for all the close-up shots. To make the cockroaches docile, they were put into a fridge for a short spell and then to perk them up again the 'handler' just blew some hot air from his hairdryer onto them. No one ever admitted how many of the damn things escaped onto the stage before we got the desired shots, but then again I guess they didn't want Julie to know some were loose on the set.

Graham Stark was a joy to work with, and he kept the crew amused all the time with tales of working with Blake and Peter Sellers on previous Pink Panthers. The film was a great success, grossing $28 million at the box office. Julie and Robert Preston picked up Oscar nominations for their roles, and the art department was nominated. However, since only two art directors could (then) be put forward with the production designer, I was asked if I would allow William Craig Smith, the Los Angeles-based art director, to get the other nomi-

nation even though he never came to England. This, it was explained, was because he had been diagnosed with cancer and they felt in the circumstances it would be nice for him. Of course I agreed. I finished up with a credit of 'assistant art director'.

My grandmother always told me everything comes equal in the end, and she was right, I went on to win an Emmy some years later.

The other nominations were for Blake's directing, costume design and music, though the only Oscar the film won was for the latter. ❑

14 Firefox (1981)

Following *Victor Victoria* I was asked by John Graysmark if I'd like to go to Vienna and work on the 'Moscow part' of the spy film *Firefox*, in which Clint Eastwood was starring, as well as producing and directing. Although much of the story was set in Russia – where our hero had to steal a highly advanced prototype Soviet jet, nicknamed 'Firefox' – the Iron Curtain was still firmly in place, and so Austria was standing in for the Russian locations. The other half of the movie, which was largely special effects, was to be shot in Los Angeles.

A few of the American unit came over for the location shoot, one being the gaffer (or head) electrician, Don Nygren. Don had heard from our local crew that you could take a catamaran down the Danube, arriving just seventy-five minutes later in the capital of Slovakia (Bratislava), where you could take a tour of the city. The attraction towards the Eastern Block, and the curiosity to peek inside, was one that always proved insatiable to the Americans. A further four of us (myself included) said we'd be interested in accompanying him the following Sunday. The trip down the

FILM CREDITS

Firefox
Director: Clint Eastwood
Stars: Clint Eastwood,
Freddie Jones

◄ Stealing the top secret plane, aka the Firefox.

▲ Clint Eastwood starred in, as well as directed, the film. Here he is just after one of the taut action scenes where he beats up a man on the public toilet set.

river, watching both the architecture and countryside change from bright and colourful to somewhat drab 'Communist' shades of grey, was very interesting and enlightening to say the least. On alighting at the Bratislava landing stage, we were met by our lady guide who immediately took all our passports – I guess to guarantee that we wouldn't wander too far away!

As she escorted us into the city, I remember thinking what a joy it was to see old cobbled streets unadorned by ugly double yellow lines, like those in London which were always such a pain for us when it came to filming period scenes. When she told us that both young Mozart and Franz Liszt had lived in this particular street, one of our group – Vic, our head painter – chirped up, saying 'Don't worry about us getting Mozart and List [*sic*], when can we go to a nice warm café?' I think his cockney rhyming slang went right over her head – thank goodness!

Our guide thought we should all go to the Novy-Most ('New') Bridge that the Communist authorities had built over the Danube to bring together all the boroughs of the city. It had a revolving café perched 80m up on two inclined legs, and I wasn't surprised to hear that it was referred to as a 'UFO', as it looks just like a flying saucer. One leg contained a small lift, the other a spiral emergency staircase of 430 steps – and I know that for a fact, because when we'd finished our coffee and cakes up there, we found a long queue waiting for the lift and since it only took seven people on each run, and with at least thirty people waiting, the crew – except for myself and the guide – headed down via the spiral stairs. Eight minutes later they reappeared, looking exhausted and recounting just how many steps they'd taken. By all accounts, the fire door at the ground level had been firmly locked, and so not only had they had to walk down 430 steps, but they had to then walk back up. Mind you, their timing was perfect as the lift arrived and its doors opened for the guide and myself. Wasn't I glad I decided to stay with our guide, and the passports!

John Graysmark got on very well with Clint, although, unlike the other crew members who would often automatically and immediately agree to anything our director suggested in a scene, John was never shy to suggest an alternative (or often, as it happened, a better) idea, which Clint actually found very refreshing. One case in point was when Clint was in the shadows of an alleyway, and said he would strike a match and light up a Cheroot to reveal his face. 'You do that on every film!' John said, 'What about an ambulance drives by with blue lights flashing to light up your face for a few seconds instead?' Clint liked it, and developed a great respect for John, appreciating that he wasn't one of 'the nodding brigade'. Consequently, they discussed a lot more of the set-ups and scenes together.

◄ In Vienna, Clint takes a look at a shot his director of photography, Bruce Surtees, has lined up.

One of the sets required a gentlemen's toilet in a railway station, where a fight was to take place. We couldn't do it in a real loo as a lot of damage was to be inflicted on wash basins, urinals etc., so we decided to build it close enough to our exterior night locations, in case we needed a wet weather cover. Permission was sought and duly given for us to build it on a large open concourse that formed part of the underground system. Sure enough, on the second night shoot it poured with rain, so the unit was moved down into the concourse set.

With the nature of any fight scene, especially as Clint was both acting and directing, it's not until it is cut together that you know 100 per cent if any further shots and close-ups are required to cut into

the scene. Hence, every time John Graysmark asked Clint, 'Can we strike the toilet set?', the reply was, 'Not yet'. This went on for a week, until one morning Clint gave me the OK to strike it whilst John was out looking for an airfield location. The construction gang went to work and the whole set was smashed up, put in trucks and sent to the city's rubbish dump in about two hours flat.

When John came back he was delighted to see the stagehands doing a final sweep-up of the area. Clint, knowing how many times John had asked him if he could strike it, decided he'd play a little gag, telling John that he only had two more pick-up shots to do that night and then he could get rid of the set. Poor John had no idea how the order to strike the set

⌃ Clint looking at a scene from the film.

'Okay, as long as I don't black out!' Well, we did loops, and all the mud from my boots and others before me found its way onto the canopy above our heads when we reached the top of the loop, only to drop all over us as we dived down to pull up level again. I felt my stomach turning over in tune with the mud, and I've never been so glad to stand on terra firma as I was that day.

I'm sure that when it was Tony's turn he told the pilot to do his worst, as I watched a fantastic display with many loops, rolls etc. He finally came down to land between two hangars, and rolled to a stop not more than 20ft from the control table set up in the field. I had climbed out of the glider on my more subdued ride looking a bit green, but Tony emerged with the biggest grin on his face. It was then I realised that I ought not to try and outdo my workmate in any sort of physical challenge.

The following weekend, I suggested we catch a train into the foothills around Vienna, and then walk for a few hours before finding a lunch stop and catching a train back later. That was all well and good, but the following week, Tony, being far more physically ambitious than I was, asked if I fancied going swimming on the Sunday. He'd heard of a good pool nearby where all the local crew recommended we should go. Having paid our entry fee, we were shown into the changing cubicle area. The entrance was through one door and exit through the opposite door to the pool. I was first to exit, and found two naked ladies brushing their hair standing in front of a row of mirrors. I backed into the changing room and banged on the wall of Tony's cubicle. 'I'm coming, what's up?' he called.

'Either they directed us into the ladies, or we are overdressed,' I replied. Knowing that group nudity was not viewed in the same restrained way as it is

had originated, and was undoubtedly wondering how the heck he was going to break the news to his director. His mind worked overtime, thinking how rebuilding even part of it would be both time-consuming and expensive. Having witnessed John suffer in silent contemplation for a few minutes, Clint walked over and started laughing. Clint, unlike many new directors on the block, likes to take the pressure of working flat out with a bit of jolly japing, and I had never seen John so relieved.

As eventful as any location is on a film, it's often your days off that prove more enlightening than anything else. I wasn't one to just sit around, so when Tony, our construction manager, and I were invited to the local gliding club to try our hand at the sport over the Austrian Alps and the old Formula One race circuit, I readily agreed. We felt we were in safe hands, as the pilot of the dual seat glider was a former world champion. When he asked me if I would like to do some aerobatics, not wanting to be a wimp I said

which was a much warmer, bath temperature – it was like swimming in a thick cloud – and finally we finished up in a sauna.

The TV show, *Game for a Laugh*, sprang to mind as we opened the large door to find almost forty naked people sitting around on all the different levels. The only available place was on the top shelf, and I could not believe how hot it was up there – like sitting in an oven at gas mark 9. As the heat built up, a well-endowed guy stood up in front of the crowd, and kept flipping his towel (and other bits) to bring the hot air from my level down to the lower section. I was grateful, but the temperature became so unbearable that, as soon as I felt the hairs in my nose begin to crinkle up with the heat, I decided it was definitely time for me to go. I climbed over all the slumped naked bodies back to floor level and opened the big pine door to leave, when all of the dedicated steam-lovers booed me out for letting their hot air escape.

I never found out if it was all a wind-up, the crew recommending we go there, or if they were genuine in asking how the swimming went. I didn't let on, though, so if they were expecting some sort of crazed reaction then they were disappointed. The only thing that I could not apply my 'take it all in your stride' attitude to was sitting in the café/bar area drinking coffee or a beer without my clothes on. I guess the hedonistic lifestyle was just not for me ...

Overall, my abiding memory of Vienna was when we were shooting along the banks of the famous Blue Danube. Blue it certainly was not. It was not just the colour, which one accepts like most rivers was a muddy brown, but it was the raw sewage floating down the river that was a bit of a shock. Luckily we never had any one fall in, as the long list of injections necessary to ward off the many waterborne diseases if you did proved to be a terrific deterrent. ❑

in England, I guessed it was the latter. Carrying our towels strategically placed in front of us, we enjoyed the new experience of swimming in the nude. Whilst clothes were forbidden, the strange thing was you could not enter the pool without a protective rubber hat. Luckily, out of the two colours available I had a dark green one, because the white ones just looked like oversized condoms!

It didn't take long to get accustomed to our state of undress, and I'm sure that going around the pool area with our clothes on would have been far more embarrassing. We joined in, trying the jacuzzi, and then swam through a glass tunnel to the outside pool

15 *Trail of the Pink Panther* (1981)

FILM CREDITS

Trail of the Pink Panther
and *The Curse of the Pink Panther*

Director: Blake Edwards
Stars: Peter Sellers,
David Niven

Another memorable recce was when I had to fly to the South of France for a Pink Panther outing. It was a bit of a surprise to get the call, to be honest, as the quite irreplaceable Peter Sellers had sadly passed away two years before. I asked who they'd cast in the role of the bumbling French detective and was told that the plan was to utilise some unseen footage from previous outings and cut them in with some new film to produce a movie about 'the search for the missing Clouseau'.

I was instructed to meet up with the French production manager in Nice and find suitable location choices for Blake Edwards to view when he flew in from LA, six days later. My production designer, Peter Mullins, would also arrive from London on the same day.

➤ Do you have a *rheum*?

◀ Blake Edwards is seen here on set with our director of photography, Ernie Day.

The night before my early morning flight from London it snowed heavily. So much so that the radio was full of warnings for blocked roads and multiple crashes. When my driver arrived on time I was frankly astonished, but he said the back roads were better than the main ones, so we should be okay as he knew a route around. Call me old-fashioned, but I like to travel looking quite smart, so there were no embla-zoned T-shirt and well-worn jeans for me. I donned my best attire, which perhaps wasn't the best of ideas as I soon found myself having to get out of the car and struggle to push the damn big Mercedes out of snowdrifts on at least four occasions.

When we reached the lanes around the flat, exposed fields near Heathrow we found the wind had blown the snow off the fields and dumped it in the road! Usually it took me about an hour to get to the airport, but on this morning we had taken well over one and a half hours and were still not there. I was beginning to get a little agitated about being late, but I needn't have worried since half the flight crews coming from London were all stuck in the traffic somewhere, too.

I checked in, and went through to the departure lounge to find another film crew also travelling out to Nice with Maggie Smith to do some extra shots on the Merchant Ivory production, *Quartet*. It was a pleasant distraction from the weather to while away the two hour delay with people I knew from previous films. We finally got away, after the runway had been

▲ The irreplaceable Peter Sellers. Quite how they hoped a Pink Panther film would work without him I'll never know.

cleared and the plane de-iced again. The white land-scape ended at Dover, and it was so nice to see green fields again over France.

In Nice, my case was one of the first to hit the conveyor belt and, as the French production office had sent a car for me, I thought I'd dash straight to my hotel, change into less formal clothes to suit climbing over rocks, etc., and get straight to work to make up for the delay. The drive from the airport was lined with coloured flowerbeds of cyclamen and mimosa trees in full bloom, and, coming from a country that was effectively closed down with bad weather, a dual carriageway bedecked with amazing flowers made it feel like a summer's day.

At the hotel I told the driver to wait, and I would be back down in ten minutes. I popped my case on the bed and opened it up, only to find a load of ladies underwear and dresses. What chance, the same case

on the same flight at the same time? So back to the airport we went, and of course the sole bag still going around the carousel was mine. I did the swap, but could not find the lady whose suitcase I had inadvertently rushed away with. This was probably just as well, since she would have known that I had seen all of her underwear for the following week!

Unfortunately, on the day we did the tour of all the proposed locations, Peter Mullins was delayed at the airport with thick fog, so I had to steer Blake around them myself. Poor Peter arrived later in the day, and chased us around to each location only to be told we'd moved on to the next. Knowing he was a difficult director to please, the fact that Blake liked four out of five of our chosen locations was judged a great success.

One was a vineyard, looking down the valley just outside Nice. Since it was the wrong time of the year to have the rows of vines in full leaf with hanging fruit, we planned to use fake leaves and fruit. For five days before the shoot we had a team dedicated to decorating the whole field, making it look like September. When Blake arrived to give it his blessing, I was so pleased to proudly show off our new vineyard to him. However, Blake turned his head across to the opposite field and suggested he thought it might be a better choice. Of course, you never argue with a director of his standing and experience, but it doesn't mean you can't scream silently in your head!

It was now Saturday afternoon and the shoot was scheduled for Monday morning, so the whole production team from both England and France were paid to work all day on Sunday to strike the original field, move it in boxes to the adjacent field and dress the vines up again. It was what we call 'a job and finish' and we finally completed it at 4.15 p.m. on Sunday, feeling absolutely exhausted. The original prop-dressing gang, who'd gone away Saturday lunchtime, had

no idea of the late change and could not believe their eyes when they reported for duty on Monday. Was it April Fool's Day, they wondered?

The highlight for me, going back to the first recce, was when we were all invited by David Niven to his villa at Cap Ferrat. Blake had wanted him to have a small part in the film, reprising his role of Sir Charles Litton from the very first Pink Panther film. I never knew, at that time, that he was in the early stages of battling with motor neuron disease. In fact, by the time we got round to filming his scenes they had to dub him, with someone else mimicking his voice. It was so sad to see such a great actor, who relished in telling the most wonderful stories (his books were proof of that, as they sold up to 6 million copies around the world), being struck down by such a hugely debilitating illness.

Mr Niven entertained us all royally, with a choice of different tea blends and some of those famous continental pastries. Sitting on his veranda looking over his pool to the open sea was one of those magic moments that make up for all the nightmares that occur when, through no fault of your own, the 'best laid plans of mice and men' (and vineyards) go awry.

During the shoot we shut down for four days for Easter, and Blake went back to Switzerland, while I decided to take the time to drive up to a new ski resort built in the mountains just eighty minutes from Nice. Amazingly, in such a short distance, you can go from sunbathing on the beach in the morning to skiing all afternoon. Whilst I was staying at my hotel there, one evening at dinner a young English lady asked if she could join me, as she did not like eating alone and she knew I was English from hearing me talking at the reception. I am always on my guard for such forward approaches, so I was relieved to hear that her fiancé was due to join her the next day; she said he was flying in from the Middle East. When I enquired 'what does he do?' she said 'he shoots people'.

'A film director?' I stupidly asked.

'No, he's a mercenary,' she replied with the same delivery as if he was a fishmonger. I felt myself pushing my chair back away from the table, and thought how lucky I was that he wasn't arriving until the next day. I was very happy to be leaving to drive back down to the safety of the crowded seafront of Nice, and away from a mercenary husband who might have got the wrong idea about seeing his wife having dinner with me.

Being a Formula One enthusiast, I often wondered how they surrounded the streets of Monaco with miles of 'Armco' barriers so quickly each year. With the race

➤ The vineyard that we had to hurriedly move.

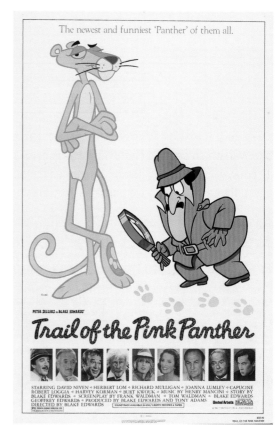

only two weeks away, I decided to take myself off down the coast and, 18 miles later and in less than an hour, I was in the lovely principality. I had timed my visit perfectly as construction of the track was already in full swing. In the gutters around the circuit are little metal covers that, with a special extractor, lift up to reveal a square hole the exact size of each of the steel uprights that take the 'Armco' lengths of crash barrier. So, after the race, it takes only a few days of striking to remove all the barriers and return the roads to normal with tourists and locals filling the streets. You would never even notice where the barriers had been. A bit like a film crew on a location ...

Anyhow, having completed the shoot we returned to the studios to finish the rest of the film. To suppress a fit of giggles during a take on a comedy is always difficult, and even more so on an Inspector Clouseau film. The scenes we did in a ground floor corridor, with Herbert Lom in an electric wheelchair with one leg wrapped in an oversized plaster cast, took all the crew to their limit. Chief Inspector Dreyfus, played by Lom, had to negotiate his wheelchair down the hallway, missing the potted indoor planters, then reverse into the lift. Naturally, when the lift doors closed, a good part of the plaster cast was still protruding. We filmed

a shot of the leg moving up the doors with dire consequences. Herbert kept asking if he could practise with the wheelchair. We were told by Blake to make up any excuse we liked, but he was not allowed to practise under any circumstances. I overheard Blake say to the operator, 'Shoot the rehearsal'.

Poor Herbert, he could never get it going in a straight line, and he crashed his way forwards and backwards until he was in the lift. Thinking it was just a rehearsal, he was amazed when Blake said, 'cut'. I, along with the rest of the crew, was in stitches and eventually burst out laughing.

The film did, of course, suffer for not having Peter starring in it, and the critics were very harsh.

16 *Memphis Belle* (1989)

Studios often remake previously successful films in the hope of further cashing in on an earlier winner. *Memphis Belle* was first described to me as being a 'remake' of a factual documentary from the Second World War, which centred on the final missions of a B-17 crew, who, against all the odds, chalked up the magical figure of twenty-five missions over enemy territory – this guaranteed them a ticket home and a tickertape reception all around the United States.

The 1944 documentary was directed by Major William Wyler, and is still considered to be one of the great factual films of the Second World War. It was very fitting that Wyler's daughter, Catherine, was at the forefront of the proposed movie. With the help

FILM CREDITS

Memphis Belle
Director: Michael Caton-Jones
Stars: Mathew Modine, Eric Stoltz

Sean Astin, who played Richard 'Rascal' Moore, talking to one of the original air crew with our producer, David Puttnam, in the background.

▲ A publicity shot of the whole crew, as portrayed by a very talented bunch of actors.

➤ The ten crew in our film, posing with their lucky dog mascot.

of Monte Merrick, they produced a very worthy first draft script set around a fictitious plane, which captured the wartime struggle and bravery of the bomber crews of the 8th Air Force.

It really all got going when Catherine joined David Puttnam, the new head of Columbia Pictures, as his vice president of film production. She put forward various ideas to develop for future feature films, and the lingering idea of the script based on her father's documentary proved too tempting not to suggest. She ran her father's film for David and he was very keen to develop the project further, as he was an avid lover of similar Second World War movies, like *Twelve O'clock High*. Sadly, however, a short time afterwards David left Columbia and returned to Britain, but the idea for a B-17 bomber crew film was not forgotten.

The script was put into 'turnaround', which is where a studio offers the rights to a project in exchange

for the money it has already spent, plus a bit of interest. David, through his own company, Enigma Productions, raised the money to buy the script and invited Catherine to come over and join him as co-producer to help push the project along. With the money raised, a crew was assembled and I was fortunate enough to be one of them!

Our first problem was in finding enough B-17 aircraft to look as though we had a squadron. Eric Rattray (production manager) and Stuart Craig (production designer) went over to the States to check out available aircraft, and to see if anywhere there could double for Middle England – to save bringing the planes across the Atlantic. They returned, saying that there were no satisfactory airfields over there,

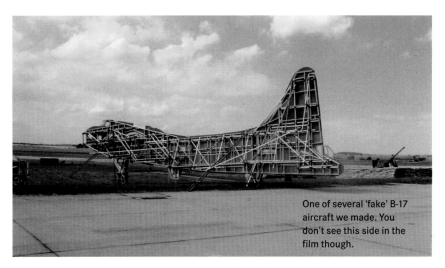

One of several 'fake' B-17 aircraft we made. You don't see this side in the film though.

and decided that the film would have be made here in Britain because, after all, this is where it happened.

Two B-17 owners were willing to fly their planes over: Bob Richardson, who had the oldest aircraft, and David Tallichet, himself a B-17 pilot who had been stationed in Norfolk during the war. These two, along with another three operational B-17s we had found in Europe, gave us the basis of our squadron. Out of the three European planes, Duxford based *Sally B* was to double up for the *Memphis Belle* herself.

Having secured the aircraft, Stuart's next task was to find an airfield that we could take over lock, stock and barrel. There is nothing worse for a director than to be told we have to wait for an inbound aircraft to land, just when he wants to get his shots done.

Stuart looked at the original home of the *Memphis Belle* at Bassingbourn, but it was then an army barracks with very heavy security in and out – I know that from just visiting the original control tower to take measurements – and it was considered too restricting for our requirements. What seemed like the reasonably straightforward task of finding a location in southern England with intact Second World War hangars, surrounded by countryside, proved a tall order, so we considered looking further afield.

Following a tip from an RAF guard who'd heard of our quest and suggested Binbrook in Lincolnshire, we investigated further.

The airfield had only recently reverted to a care-and-maintenance base – that is to say, it was closed as an operational base but open for the odd emergency landing, and was covered by a small standby crew. It ticked all the boxes, and even had the C-type hangars that matched the Bassingbourn ones, along

◄ A selfie, for my album!

▲ Bombing up on a wet morning.

∧ This wonderful metal mock-up of the interior was all made in the Pinewood carpenter's shop. The bomb rack (complete with numbers) came over from the USA for us to build into the set.

➤ Taken from Binbrook's control tower roof, showing the arrival of the B-17s from RAF Duxford.

with several wartime Nissen huts that could be easily incorporated into the film's background.

Once permission was given by the Ministry of Defence, we all moved up to Lincolnshire. I was based in Grimsby, about 9 miles away, and the drive through the countryside each morning during the summer was a delight. One of the assistant directors started to put stickers of rabbit and hedgehog kills on the side of his sports car to mirror the bombing runs of our B-17 squadron. Mind you, I think he may have been exaggerating after the first two!

The existing modern control tower was still RAF-manned for the very occasional visits of aircraft, so removing it was not an option. We figured the only way to keep it operational was to build our wartime control tower around the outside, to hide all their modern rooftop equipment. The big lighting gantries were removed, and more grass was laid directly onto the concrete to give the impression of less space around the tower. The turf, laid on sand, kept drying out because the heat coming up from the concrete

taxi areas was tremendous, so we had to water it regularly throughout the day.

Stuart Craig asked me to prepare a full set of working drawings of the inside of the plane. As it was such a mammoth job, Michael Lamont, another aeroplane enthusiast, came on board to share the task. We were allowed four visits to photograph and measure Duxford's non-flying B-17, *Mary Alice*, which was deemed to have the most authentic interior.

At that point, our director, Michael Caton-Jones, came along to see how restricting it was going to be to film ten actors within a 7ft diameter tapering tube. To his credit, and despite the cameraman undoubtedly wanting to open the space up, he felt he needed to keep it exactly as it was to convey every aspect of what those guys had to endure, with the cold and the cramped conditions. It was all part of the experience and danger he wanted to relate, and the incoming flak from fighters over Europe only served to heighten it all. This, happily for me, also meant that the available items coming over from the States, such as bomb racks, radio units etc., would fit perfectly.

Michael Lamont and I divided up the fuselage into six areas, and we both took a section to draw on each of our Duxford visits. We knew that we'd have to make the whole plane in sheet metal, as plywood was not

How low can you go?

➤ The foreground miniature we created of the whole squadron waiting to take off.

going to be strong enough, particularly as we had to construct the whole plane to go on a large gimbal that rocked it violently. We also needed the ability to 'float away' whole pieces of each side to allow room for wider angles and lamps.

The nose section was constructed outside the studio by the Mo Gomme company, who specialised in fabricating racing car body shells. They had the craftsmen and equipment to bend the metal into the nose-shape.

The main fuselage, meanwhile, was built in the carpenter's shop at Pinewood, with the crew using rivet guns instead of hammers and saws for a change!

Whilst Binbrook was our main location, the base for our five B-17s was Duxford, where they were used to old aeroplanes that needed constant support and engineering backup facilities.

On 16 July, the big day, our bomber fleet flew in from Duxford to Binbrook, but because we had positioned

our full size B-17 cut-outs around the airfield, the pilots could not believe where all these other aircraft had come from. Brian Bishop, one of our top scenic artists, had painted them all, and his forte was placing various pieces of cooking foil to reflect the light naturally onto shiny surfaces such as the wings and cockpit panels, thereby enhancing the 3D effect for what was just a flat piece of painted plywood. When viewed from a distance it was hard to tell the real plane from the cut-out!

We were blessed with a wonderful technical adviser, Roger Freeman, who offered so much valuable input during the preparation period to ensure the whole film looked authentic. Having spent his life studying all the American bomber bases in the UK, and with many publications to his credit, it put him right at the top for knowledge of the 8th Air Force. He had amassed a photo archive of 10,000 pictures – some in colour – and I was able to visit his house and go through his many albums. His whole collection is now part of the Imperial War Museum's archive. A good technical advisor is so valuable to a period production, and I can't praise the commitment he gave to the film enough.

I have often said that working around B-17s and Second World War vehicles all day was a job I'd probably have done for free. In fact, I often spotted other enthusiasts on the far side of the airfield looking with binoculars and zoom lenses through the outer fence, and I pinched myself that here I was in the middle of it all.

On one occasion, I was asked to direct one of the bombers up to the far side of the airfield and park it in an area we had constructed near to a cornfield, ready for the scenes when our hero (played by Matthew Modine) helps a local farmer repair his horse-drawn threshing machine. I will never forget looking in my rear-view mirror to see this big bomber with all four engines running, following me around the peri-track up to the 'frying pan' hard standing.

Eventually, I went one better when I was able to fly in one of the B-17s for about twenty minutes. I sat in the bomb aimer's position, which was about the best view you could have for take-offs and landings, and on climbing out of the plane afterwards I remember thinking I would like to have another trip up in near future. Unfortunately, the very next day any thought of quick

▲ The hydraulic rocker unit for the interior shots on the Pinewood sound stages.

joyrides ended with a major crash and the total loss of the aircraft, but thankfully the crew and passengers escaped with no more than one fractured leg and a broken collar bone. It was a miracle no one was killed.

It was actually at lunchtime when the accident occurred, and marked the first time we heard the emergency sirens going. Running out from the catering area, we could see the smoke rising up from the crash site and an RAF firefighting Land Rover rushed past. At that point I realised the amount of water he could carry was very limited and, as we had a full tanker of water parked up for watering our 'golf tee quality' turfed area, I ran to the cab but couldn't start it. John Sargeant, our head of transport, jumped in and got it going and we drove as fast as we could to the crash site. When time is of the essence, you just want to get there as soon as possible in case lives are at stake, so John drove through a 5ft high hedge at full speed, but had not realised there was an old drainage ditch on the far side. Not having a steering wheel to hold onto and no seat belt, I went up in the air and crashed into the roof of the cab as we hit the ditch. John shoved it into reverse and I had about thirty seconds to recover before we arrived at the crash site. I staggered out of the cab and immediately fell over – so much for me helping to save people!

The only other joy flight we let go up after that was when six of the original *Memphis Belle* crew members arrived with their wives, all paid for by Enigma Productions. When airborne they allowed one of them, Bob Morgan, to take the controls for a while and he said it was the first time since 1945 that he'd flown in a B-17. When asked what it felt like afterwards, he said 'it was like five Christmases all on the same day'.

I was due to finish at the end of the location period, because during my four weeks of preparation and four weeks shooting on location, the interior set of the *Memphis Belle*, plus other Nissen hut sets had been completed in the studio. I must admit I felt a bit like a surrogate mother handing over my baby, although I did get visiting rights at the studio on many occasions until 6 October, when it was all in the can.

The interior of the *Memphis Belle* set was, incidentally, shipped to an Australian museum after filming, for people to walk through and experience the restrictions endured by the ten crew members.

I hope the film will show future generations what these brave young airmen did, and I feel proud to have been part of it. ❏

17 *Robin Hood: Prince of Thieves* (1990)

In the late 1980s it seemed time for another big screen version of the legendary Robin Hood and his band of merry men. Many television adaptations had come and gone, but with a decent budget and starring Kevin Costner and Morgan Freeman, and with Kevin Reynolds directing, we were all set for a no-expense-spared interpretation of the story.

My old friend, John Graysmark, was the production designer, and it goes without saying that I was very pleased when he asked me to join him on the adventure.

Our first job was to make a card model of the big set to be constructed on the backlot at Shepperton Studios. This was primarily the inside of Nottingham Castle with its surrounding battlements, and also the exterior of a church.

We then began looking for forest areas within commuting distance of the studio, where we could construct Robin Hood's secret camp. Our first port of call was Burnham Beeches, but although Kevin Reynolds liked it he thought there could be something 'a bit different' elsewhere, so I was dispatched to explore most of the woods and forests in southern England! My search eventually led me to the New Forest in Hampshire where, indeed, I found something just 'a

FILM CREDITS

Robin Hood: Prince of Thieves (Supervising Art Director)
Director: Kevin Reynolds
Stars: Kevin Costner, Alan Rickman

◀ Kevin Costner really threw himself into the action scenes.

▲ Yours truly, posing on the battlements of the Nottingham Castle keep and church set.

little bit different' from the thousands of trees I had looked at everywhere else. Here, deep in the forest, I came across three enormous ash trees that had been blown down in the hurricane of 1987. They lay like the bleached bones of some prehistoric monster, with the bowl of their torn-up roots leaving a big pit with an upright earth wall, a bit like a fallen wine glass. These pits would be easy to convert to living quarters

for the outlaws, I thought, with long branches and animal skins.

Thankfully, Kevin Reynolds loved the idea, and decided the first camp (where Robin meets and joins forces with the outlaws) should be here, with one of the fallen trees used for Robin to hold court over the motley band of men. At the next production meeting it was agreed that the second, more general, camp would utilise Burnham Beeches. Here, the outlaws were to have catwalks and houses up in the trees. However, our construction manager, completely out of the blue, said it would be impossible to build platforms amongst the trees because when the wind blew they would all move in different directions, leading to the platforms being dislodged.

Well, I knew if the script said 'tree houses', then tree houses we would have to supply. I told our very dejected director not to worry, we'd overcome this obstacle. I didn't want to embarrass the construction manager at the meeting, so afterwards I explained my idea to overcome the problems by constructing the main tree house platforms on scaffold supports, covering them with dummy bark to represent tree trunks and setting them close to two or three real big trees. The platforms around these could then move back and forth over the fixed platforms on which the houses were built.

What fun it was to construct the tree houses out of sawn timber and plywood, then cover them in branches we had gathered from the woods. Thankfully, we had a big supply of Scottish heather wired up in big rolls, so it was easy to clad over the walls and roofs.

Kevin Reynolds had walked Hadrian's Wall as a student and loved that part of Northumberland's wild landscape with its stunning views. So, he sent me up there to find the location for the sequence where Robin and Azeem save a boy from the Sheriff of Nottingham's men when he is caught up a tree. My quest was to find a tree with stunning views that could easily be climbed by a young boy. It sounds easy until you start to recce the 84 miles of Roman wall!

The wild and windy open country up there has few trees; it's mostly scrubland. The few woods there are plantation fir trees. I was about to return home when I came across one solitary (and easily climbable) tree

▲ The set was constructed on the Shepperton Studios backlot.

in a natural dip of the land. I read a plaque under the tree that said it had been planted as a memorial to a particular lady's husband, as this had been their favourite picnic spot. It looked so perfect for a young boy to scramble up into, so I photographed it from all angles and we subsequently applied to the local authorities for the clearance to film there. Mind you, we had a fight on our hands convincing them we wouldn't do any damage to the Roman wall or the surrounding area. Nowadays, if you walk that part of the wall, the tree which is known as the 'sycamore gap' is an additional tourist attraction with another plaque saying: 'This is the tree as used in the film *Robin Hood: Prince of Thieves*'.

For Maid Marian's abbey, we decided on Hulne Abbey within the private grounds of the Duke of Northumberland's estate. It was mostly in ruins, apart from the chapel which had been converted into a flat for the head gamekeeper to the duke. When the gamekeeper died, the duke allowed the gamekeeper's daughter to stay as long as she wanted.

▲ Director Kevin Reynolds on location in the New Forest. He liked the trees I'd found.

➤ When I was applying for a work permit in the USA, Kevin Reynolds kindly wrote a letter of support.

'Prince of Thieves' Productions Limited

22 November 1990

To whom it may concern:

I would like to take this opportunity to express what a personal and professional pleasure it is to work with someone of Alan Tomkins' stature. He is one of the most talented Art Directors in the business today and has the ability to work under tremendous pressure without losing his perspective.

It would be a great help in my future projects were I able to use Alan in the United States and hope that in some way my letter will help expedite his getting a work permit and eventual guild membership.

Alan and I are currently working on the Morgan Creek/ Warner Bros. project entitled "Robin Hood - Prince of Thieves" starring Kevin Costner and filming in England and France. Alan's art direction has given this movie a medieval feel far beyond what I had hoped for. His untiring research and interest in achieving an accurate depiction of that era, shows in every scene we have shot.

If there is any way I can be of further assistance, please do not hesitate to contact me either here in the U.K. or in the United States care of Morgan Creek Productions.

Kind regards,

Kevin H. Reynolds
Director

Lee International Studios Shepperton,
Studios Road,
Shepperton, Middlesex. TW17 0QD
Tel: (0932) - 562611
Fax: (0932) - 564765 (Production Office)
Fax: (0932) - 569989 (Shepperton Studios)

1875 Century Park East.
Suite 200
Los Angeles, CA 90067
Tel: (213) - 284 - 8884
Fax: (213) - 282 - 8794

Registered in England No: 2503974   Registered Office: Hanover House. 14 Hanover Square, London W1R 0BE

We rebuilt some of the ruins to suit the script requirements, and my wife and I became friendly with the occupier of the chapel flat. Having told her that our hotel in Alnwick was very dirty, she offered us the guest room, which suited me as I was able to get up and be on set in a few minutes. A nice change.

One looming problem was the fact that any fires lit in Burnham Beeches had to be under strict safety guidelines, so we knew that shooting fireballs and flaming arrows through the woods was never going to be allowed there. Luckily, that's when word came back that we could construct some tree houses in the woods belonging to the Duke of Northumberland, who was so pleased with our presence that he gave us the OK to shoot flaming arrows to our hearts' content.

Our construction manager came up with a team to construct the extra tree houses, and all went well until we returned from lunch one day to find that a brand new power generator, which had been purchased for location use, had vanished. Now, we were in private woods on a private estate, so you would have thought that our construction equipment would be safe, especially as the bulky generator took two men to lift. I thought it might have been hidden close by or buried, but we never found anything. Another unsolved mystery.

I should mention that, being interested in all aspects of the history of D-Day I was surprised to find, in almost all of the woods and forests I investigated in southern England, that there were large concrete slabs hidden deep in the trees. These were all laid down early in 1944 for huts or latrines with which to support the drivers of the hundreds of vehicles

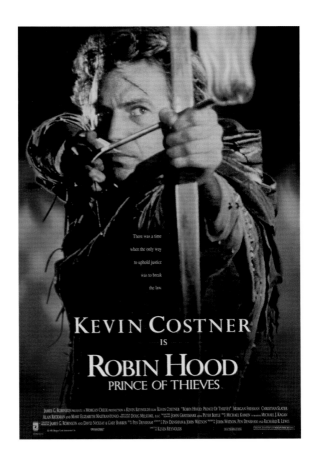

and that iconic shot (now often copied) of the arrow speeding into the tree was set up.

Having found those early locations on Hadrian's Wall and in the New Forest, I'm afraid I made a rod for my own back, as Kevin did not trust anyone other than me to find all the remaining Sherwood locations. Mind you, it was fun exploring all that countryside on foot – something I would never have time to do ordinarily. Sadly, my boss and good friend, John Graysmark, was too busy with building all the sets in the studio and on the backlot to have time to join me on those forays, but he was happy that I was keeping our director content.

When it came to the final wedding of Robin to Maid Marian, Peter Young, our set decorator, added lots of artificial berries into our ornamental arches, made with big, ivy-clad branches. It was all to look extra special, you see, because Sean Connery had agreed to star in a one-day guest appearance (for an undisclosed fee that would go to a charity in Scotland – rumoured to be $1 million). He would play King Richard in a pivotal role in the ceremony. The prop boys had done a great job building an altar out of the branches they had gathered, and all was set for the big scene.

'Can you paint Sean Connery's name on the chair back?', I was asked. Signwriting on canvas is not easy, and I would be the first to admit I'm not a signwriter, so I came up with the next best thing – I painted a king's crown on the chair back, which Sean loved, thank goodness. Sometimes thinking totally out of the box pays off!

The film premiered on 13 June 1991, and on its first weekend grossed $25 million in the US, followed by $390 million globally. It certainly made all that standing around in the rainy English countryside and feeling miserable, well worth it. ❏

which were all hidden under the tree canopies to stop enemy planes photographing the massive build-up of tanks and vehicles.

Throughout the many weeks filming in Burnham Beeches, Kevin Reynolds often asked me to meet him at 7 a.m. to walk the woods looking for other Sherwood Forest locations: for the stealing of the Sheriff's taxes scene, or the capture of Maid Marian. We often set out with barely enough light to see one tree from the other. One of the toughest of all to find was a flat clear area of 100ft, in which to lay a camera track running into a decent sized tree trunk. A spinning arrow head was placed in front of the camera,

18 The Oliver Stone Trilogy: *JFK*, *Heaven & Earth* and *Natural Born Killers* (1991–94)

FILM CREDITS

JFK
Director: Oliver Stone
Stars: Kevin Costner, Gary Oldman

Heaven & Earth (Supervisor Art Director)
Director: Oliver Stone
Stars: Takaaki Enoki, Masahiko Tsugawa

Natural Born Killers
(Supervising Art Director)
Director: Oliver Stone
Stars: Woody Harrelson, Juliette Lewis

At the start of 1991, I received a call from production designer Michael Seymour, with whom I had worked for a few months the previous year during the preparation for the first *Alien*.

It was whilst working on that film that I heard this great sound coming out of one of the open stages at Shepperton, and discovered that The Who were rehearsing and setting up sound levels. They also had these new laser light beams bouncing around the

stage. I told Michael Seymour that the light beams would look great hovering over the eggs in the egg chamber set, and Michael took the idea to Ridley Scott. I left long before the egg chamber scenes were shot, so it was a pleasant surprise when I saw the film and noticed that my idea had been taken up.

My helpfulness had obviously stuck in Michael's mind, as he wanted me to go with him to Mexico to work on a film entitled *Universal Soldier*, but he said

➤ We transformed the frontage of the Book Depository with the addition of polystyrene sunscreen 'bricks'.

that all the early preparation would be done in LA – 'Tinsel Town' itself. What a wonderful opportunity to work in Hollywood, I thought, and I was really excited to see how different it was to the UK. Needless to say, everything was done on a much bigger scale.

I started working on a model of the oil rig that would form a major part in the film, and shortly afterwards Michael left with our writer/director to recce the locations in Mexico. We kept in touch, with me sending my drawings and photos of the model oil rig for discussions with the director.

The morning after their return I sensed things were not quite right, as Michael's usual positive and pleasant attitude had changed, and all he would say was 'at 10 a.m. there will be a meeting with the whole crew'. All possible scenarios were bounced around the office, but one thing was for certain – it was not going to be good news. The bottom line was, the writer/director had left the picture, taking his script with him, and the producers were putting the picture back six months, so we were all under notice. One brave soul asked when we would have to finish. This prompted the producer to look at his watch and say, 'how about now?'

Having paid for my airfare out, Michael was hugely embarrassed that it had turned out this way on my

◄◄ A new canopy and ticket office were constructed at the former cinema building.

◄ We had to lift sets into the Book Depository building, and one floor above where it all happened.

first job in Hollywood, but I told him it wasn't his fault – that's just how things go sometimes.

Back at the hotel I told my wife the news that we needed to pack and head home the next day, but she asked that I hang on until she had rung a friend of hers who was living in LA. We duly received an invitation to stay with her for a couple of weeks before returning to England, so at least we could turn what was bad luck into a bit of good luck with a holiday.

Meanwhile Michael, racked with guilt about my situation, contacted an English set decorator whom he knew was working in Dallas on Oliver Stone's *JFK*. Unfortunately they had been going for a few weeks, and all positions in the art department were taken.

⌃ A model in our workshop, with added Hertz clock.

➤ The actual location (that's me in the white cap).

Unbeknown to us, however, when the news became known that an art director (i.e. yours truly) was looking for work, the current art director, who was not only missing his family but admitted to being 'a bit terrified' of Oliver Stone, asked if he could leave, with the hope I would take over his job. I received a call later the same day, and spoke to the production designer, Victor Kempster, who asked me to fax my CV over. It would seem that the normal format of a résumé in the American film business is restricted to credits for only the prior two years. Not knowing this, I sent all the films I had worked on since leaving my parent studio and going off to Jordan on *Lawrence of Arabia*, way back in 1961. The many pages whirring off their fax machine created some amusement, but it certainly got me started two days later! Victor said he was so impressed that he wanted to take time out to come to the airport to greet me in person.

We went straight to the Stoneleigh – a very nice hotel – and I was shown to what must have been the best suite in the place. From the bathroom at one end, through the entrance hall, lounge, dining room and to the kitchen measured 85ft wall to wall! I left my wife to unpack (as I'm kind like that), and went off to meet the current art director who was making good his departure in two days' time. It wasn't long for me to pick up three weeks of previous work, but with the help of English set decorator, Crispian Sallis (son of actor Peter Sallis), I settled into the job very happily.

First up was a recce to New Orleans, where our second unit base was to be located. It's a very exciting city, and with Victor (who had been there many times before) as our guide, the evenings were full of outings to great restaurants and jazz bars including the famous Preservation Hall.

Our first job was to alter the old abandoned Wildlife & Fisheries building into the offices and corridor of New Orleans District Attorney, Jim Garrison. The lovely building had been empty for some time, but it was ideal for us to have the freedom to alter each office and decorate them with rich mahogany panelling as fitting for a DA.

The film covered Jim Garrison's investigation and prosecution of local, prominent business and society guy, Clay L. Shaw. I found out, to my cost, just how popular Shaw was locally when I went to purchase hundreds of dollars' worth of new brass handles and finger plates for the doors we were putting in to replace the existing half glass ones. Having found the best shop in town, I went through their catalogue choosing various items, and when the pile of door furniture was stacking up on the counter the owner asked me what it was for. When I said that it was for the new Oliver Stone film, *JFK*, and in particular for Jim Garrison's office, he said that he didn't want to deal with the film, as Clay Shaw was a good friend of his. And there was me hoping for a discount – I finished up with nothing! So I had to source another shop, and quickly worked out that if I was asked what all this ironmongery was for, I would say some renovations in my aunt's house on Orleans Street.

Having completed my work in New Orleans, I flew back to Dallas to prepare other scenes that would be shot in and around that city. The floor where the alleged shooting took place in the Texas School Book Depository was occupied, but we were given the use of the empty floor above; the only snag being that the windows on the floor below were circular headed, and they weren't on ours. So we made inserts to match (see photos on p. 121). All of the scenery had to be built and craned up to enter the building through the top floor window, as they would not allow us to use the lift. They really didn't want us there at all, it seemed to us.

I had heard about the 'grassy knoll', but had no idea how it linked to the shooting and its geography. I felt that I wasn't alone in this, so suggested to Oliver Stone that a model might be used in the courtroom with which Garrison could point out the order of events. Oliver loved the idea and told me to get a price

▲ Oliver Stone talks through the 'late night TV show' scene with Kevin Costner.

for it. I went to a local architectural model-building company and the price came back at $30,000. Oliver declined, saying it was far too expensive. I thought it was an important plot element and was not prepared to give up so easily. I decided to build two thirds of the model myself. All that remained to be added were the three main blocks of offices, including the Texas School Book Depositary. I also planned to build the giant Hertz billboard and electronic clock that had been on the roof at the time of the assassination (see photo on p. 122). Having obtained a new price of $8,000 on what was left to do, I was sure I would get the go ahead ...

There comes a time in everyone's life when you find yourself so carried away and committed to an idea that words come out of your mouth over which you seemingly have no control. So when Oliver said 'no' again, I heard myself saying that I would give the go-ahead, and if he didn't use it I would pay for it all myself. I quietly wished my mouth had stayed shut!

➤ Our recreation of the motorcade driving by the Book Depository.

But buoyed by the knowledge that actors generally like to work with props, especially in scenes in courtrooms to link the timescale of events to the model, I was pretty confident I would not lose the $8,000 from my salary. Sure enough, Kevin Costner made full use of it in those courtroom scenes and I breathed a sigh of relief.

Sequences showing Kennedy's body in the autopsy room were recreated by a Canadian prosthetics guy, whose company, FXsmith Inc., produced the most detailed body I had ever seen. Every hair on his body, his arms and legs were close-up perfect, and even the lighter skin tone where his watch had been was not forgotten. More out of curiosity than continuity, Susan

our 'script girl' joined us to check over the prosthetics and made just one comment: 'he was a well-endowed man'. Mr Smith, taking this as an adverse comment to the size of his manhood, coolly said 'in Canada that size is well below average'. At that point we nearly lost her to a trip to Vancouver (see photo on p. 128)!

On leaving the set that night, on a new outer city road scheme I ended up in the wrong lane, turned right into a 'no right turn' lane, and dented the side of a big limo belonging to a local oil company. I confessed it was my fault to the policeman who'd arrived within a few minutes, and my feeble excuse was that I had just seen a work colleague dead in the mortuary at the hospital, and I was not concentrating. Luckily

he did not ask me for the dead colleague's name, though he still wrote out a traffic violation slip for me to appear before a judge the following week.

It turned out that the judge was the same one the film company were dealing with, and we were in the process of upgrading his courtroom with some nice oak panelling, which he wanted us to leave after filming. Since I had been dealing with the judge's secretary previously, I asked her advice on my traffic fine. I had been told it could be up to $400, so I was relieved when she said she would speak to the judge to see if she could arrange a minimum fine for me. I arrived in the small fines courtroom, and the judge's secretary kindly met me. Bypassing a queue of other offenders, she took me through 'the wicket gate', and whispered something to the judge. He summoned me forward and asked 'would $40 be OK?' I paid up and left as soon as I could, just in case he changed his mind.

In striving to recreate Jim Garrison's office as authentically as possible, we were put in touch with

▲ Supporting actor, Donald Sutherland.

➤ Erecting the old road signs.

➤➤ My wife, Titti, admiring all the original road signs we put up after studying old photographs of the area.

the present New Orleans District Attorney, Harry Connick, through my 'friend' the judge. He was more than helpful in offering many props and portraits of past district attorneys to dress our set with. When I told him that the year before I had been working with his son (Harry Connick Jr) who was one of the *Memphis Belle* crew in the film of the same name, he wanted to hear more about the filming, and kindly invited myself and my wife out to dinner the following

Saturday. He was a well-known figure, and walking to the restaurant he was constantly stopped by people who wanted to shake his hand. Unsurprisingly, we had one of the best tables in the restaurant. He also kindly sent us all tickets for his son's concert in the New Orleans Superdome later that month.

On another occasion, we had one scene we could not find a location for. It was a small scene in a living room, and all our suggestions were rejected – either the room was too small or the ceiling was too low. Eventually, with only two days to go before filming was scheduled, we found a house furnished throughout with 1960s style furniture. The owners had sadly died in a car crash and the children had kept it all as it was, so very little was needed in the way of props.

CAMERAS ROLL—BUT NOT TRAFFIC

The Kennedy motorcade is re-created Monday on Elm Street in front of the old Texas School Book Depository for Oliver Stone's movie "JFK."

Crowds clamor for a look
at history in the re-making

Oliver came in his lunch hour with the lighting cameraman – from experience it was not the best of plans to get a positive acceptance – but they all agreed it was OK, and walked past me to leave. I was trying to blend in to the wallpaper, but as he passed Oliver wheeled around, pointed to me and said 'What would you have done if we did not like it?' I knew he was trying to catch me out, so I said, 'I have a truck full of sixties furniture, as I've been led to believe your penthouse suite in the hotel would work well!' I was told afterwards that they had never seen Oliver stumped for a cutting reply, or more likely a rebuke. I think he came to respect, and perhaps even like me.

In 1963, a massive 'Hertz Rent-a-Car' and 'Chevrolet' billboard covered two thirds of the roof of the Texas School Book Depository. At the end nearest to Dealey Plaza, there was a large electronic clock and temperature reading (see photo on p. 122). It was found out that in strong winds the sign was damaging the structure of the roof and it was taken down a few years later.

I thought a long shot of the building, with the old clock, would be useful to build the tension up to the time of the assassination at 12.30 p.m. Since CGI had not yet been invented, I suggested lining up a

◀ We made the local news.

▲ Mr Thompson didn't want his name appearing in the film, so I modified it to mine!

long shot onto a detailed photo, taken from ground level looking up, putting the built Hertz billboard and electronic clock in model form slightly set back (see set-up photo, p. 122). The model clock was filmed at different times set out by Oliver Stone. When we ran our rushes, no one could understand how we had managed to shoot it with very little expense or building. Now it would be done with a more expensive CGI shot – that's progress!

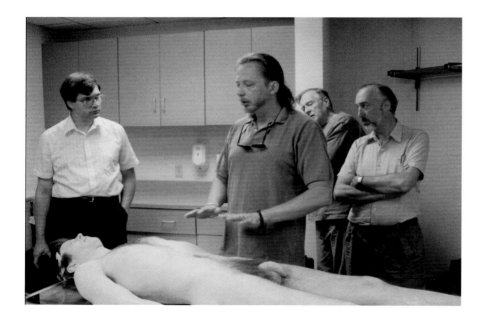

▲ Kennedy's body arrives at the local hospital, with Robert J. Groden (technical advisor) and prosthetics master, FXsmith.

Whilst in Dallas, I was asked to visit Lee Harvey Oswald's rooming house at 1026 North Beckley, as we were planning to reconstruct part of the house for the film. The owner, Mrs Roberts, showed us his old room and surprised us by saying that she had kept all the original bedroom furniture from 1963, and it was all stored in her garage, even the original fly-screen door was stored there. These, of course, were invaluable to recreating the authentic settings.

On a similar note, the lunch room that Lee Harvey Oswald was found in after the shooting, was on the second floor of the Texas School Depository Building. He was found, by Officer Marrion Baker, sitting eating his lunch. Since we planned to recreate this room from police photos taken at the time as part of a 'crime scene', I was excited to find that all the original cabinets, in the original pink colour, were still in storage in the basement. Having pulled them out, we were able to integrate them into our film set.

It was whilst filming in Dallas that one of those incredible coincidences in life occurred, with odds of millions to one. Whilst preparing for *Memphis Belle*, the production designer, Stuart Craig, recommended a book that gave a true account of pilots arriving in England in November 1942, and completing twenty-five missions in a B-17 over Europe. The book was entitled *Combat Crew* by John Comer. I had now bored the pants off Victor Kempster about this book, and I was determined to find a copy for him whilst I was in America.

The airport scenes in the film were going to be shot at Love Field Airport, the smaller of the two main Dallas airfields; they even had a row of 1960s check-in

◄ Kevin Costner with my model in the courtroom.

◄◄ That same model under construction.

desks, though admittedly not in use any more. I was sent to take measurements and photos in order to add new 1960s signage to the check-in desk area. As I was about to leave to return to the office, I noticed a sign, 'Aviation Museum and Bookshop'. I paid my entrance fee, but knew I would only give the small museum area a cursory visit, as I was desperate to ask for the book.

The white-haired gentleman behind the book counter was running the whole place on his own, and I was his only customer. 'Do you have a copy of *Combat Crew* by John Comer?' I asked. I was both surprised and delighted when he said he had, though his next question didn't sink in at first: 'Would you like me to sign it?' This man was indeed John Comer, and he only helped out on Thursday mornings at the museum!

The last location on *JFK* was probably the best. Although I enjoyed New Orleans and Dallas,

➤ Here we are transforming the shop fronts to 1963.

Washington, with all its historic landmarks was tops. There, Donald Sutherland played a 'Mr X' character, whose real name was L. Fletcher Prouty (Col. USAF Ret.). He was part of a team who were called upon to prepare briefings for the CIA on highly classified subjects, and indeed was involved in the planning and security of President Kennedy's trip to Dallas.

I had worked with Donald in Zimbabwe the previous year, on a film called *A Dry White Season*, which was about the Soweto race riots of 1976 during the South African apartheid system and co-starred Marlon Brando. I had the chance to join Donald as he was sitting on the steps of the Lincoln Memorial, and our conversation turned to our time in Zimbabwe. I asked what he thought of Marlon Brando receiving an Oscar nomination for the very small part he played in the film (which was actually shot at Pinewood at the tail end of the shoot). He looked at me and very guardedly said, 'The Academy works often in strange ways'. His statement seemed to reflect something that the character he was playing in *JFK* might say, and it was made particularly memorable as we were being overlooked by the big, seated figure of Abraham Lincoln.

I had not long returned home from Washington when Victor Kempster rang to ask if I would like to go to Thailand on Oliver Stone's next project, set against the war in Vietnam, called *Heaven & Earth*. It was the true story of a Vietnamese girl from a small village caught up in the war, her name being Le Ly Hayslip.

So, like a regular soldier, I packed my kit, and with my wife travelled out to Thailand. Le Ly came to Thailand early on, to help us get all the Vietnam village houses and gardens looking as she remembered. My wife and I were asked to meet her at the airport which, on reflection, seemed odd since the whole film was about her, and she should have had someone more high profile than me to greet her. But it was a pleasure nonetheless.

My first job was to build a village in a vast area of rice paddy fields. However, I soon lost my Thai construction manager after he said it was impossible to put the roads in because the monsoon season was upon us, so he stormed off (if you'll forgive the pun)! I remember sitting on the side of the rice paddy thinking to myself, 'You have a big unit from Hollywood arriving in twelve weeks to film in a village and you cannot even get anyone to build the roads, let alone the village'.

◄ The French armoured car I had to hastily 'acquire', undergoing a hasty build.

▼ And here it is on set.

Thankfully, the Thai production supervisor, Santa Pestoni, found someone who was prepared to take the job on, monsoon or no monsoon, though when I heard his past film experience was limited to organising the toilets, I wasn't exactly instilled with enthusiasm. However, sure enough, the next day bulldozers started to cut the roads, and tipper trucks with rubble followed on. At last things were starting to take shape.

In constructing the first of the houses, I employed four local lads who could read my drawings and transfer the sizes, and after one week all was going to plan. But then, the following Monday only two carpenters turned up for work. When I enquired what had happened to the other two guys, they answered, '*morte*'. I did not have to have that translated!

∧∧ Le Ly Hayslip at a local village.

∧ Director Oliver Stone enjoying a relaxed moment at the end of filming.

the idea of sending a telegram to the LA office, 'Half of workforce murdered at weekend, are you sure we are in the right place?'

It was very sad that a film location had been the catalyst for two murders.

The weather, meanwhile, was appalling and all the remaining rice paddies flooded immediately, so walking along the narrow raised paths between each field was the order of the day, whilst watching out for the snakes that often used to come out to sun themselves on the paths. The one good thing with the monsoon rains was that whatever you planted in the gardens, whether banana trees or vegetable crops, all grew at an amazing rate. So much so that, when the unit finally finished the LA shoot and arrived in Thailand, a lot of the crew thought the village had always been there.

With adverse weather, long days and tricky location access it proved to be a tough shoot, and we always looked forward to our Sunday rest day – relaxing on the hotel beach and swimming in the lovely warm sea, followed by lazy long lunches.

Halfway through the film, Oliver asked if we could supply a French armoured car for a refugee scene to be shot in five or six weeks' time. The chance of finding something like that in Thailand was nil, and even if one could be found in Europe, by the time it was cleared as a vintage military vehicle with the correct Carnet and shipped, it would be too late.

Well, I love a challenge like this. I rang my military vehicle man back in England and found two photos of a Renault armoured car from circa 1961. The photos were sent special delivery, and four days later I was drawing up plans to build an armoured car on an existing chassis and engine of the same wheelbase. Three weeks later we drove the armoured car (with police escort) from our workshop to the set. When Oliver

It transpired they had shot each other dead over an argument about who had the rights to take tourists out to 'James Bond Island' (so named after it was used in *The Man with the Golden Gun*). I toyed with

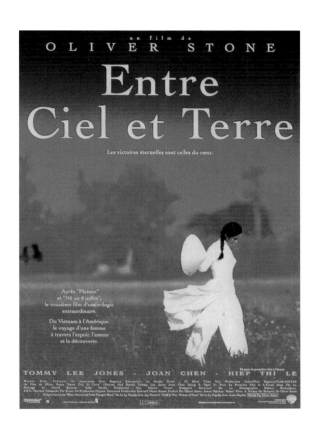

◄ There's no doubting our director was 'one hell of a man'!

outside in the bushes, using the best leaf available. We don't often stop to think how poor people living in basic accommodation manage without the modern luxuries we take for granted.

When I asked her who she thought the good guys were, since the French, then the Viet Cong and then the Americans has all trashed their village, which incidentally was close to the border between north and south. 'Alan', she said matter-of-factly, 'they were all bad guys'.

Her brother had, in fact, been talked into joining the Viet Cong, so the family saw very little of him during those troubled times. One day, a large snake with milky eyes was found in the hut and her mother believed it was the soul of her son come home to die. They dug a grave alongside the grave of their father outside the hut, and, sure enough, by the next morning the snake had crawled into the grave and died. They later found out that the son had been captured by the Americans and died in captivity.

When I returned to England I took a well-earned holiday and then decided to look for work. In the fickle world of a freelance film technician, you only have to be away for a year and you are off the radar screens of people you regularly get employment from. So I was

saw it painted up with all the correct markings he was delighted – and I think I even detected a hint of surprise that we had pulled it off. It's one of the great pleasures of my job when something like that comes off.

Le Ly Hayslip co-authored the two memoirs on which the film was based, though by then she was living in California with her three sons. She helped build several health clinics in Vietnam through the East Meets West Foundation. I will never forget two conversations I had with her. The first was when she managed, with the help of the film company, to bring her mother over to Thailand from Vietnam. She told me that her mother found it strange to do her toilet requirements inside the hotel bathroom. Having never travelled outside of her village, she always went

⌃ Woody Harrelson on the prison set.

more than delighted to get another call from Victor Kempster, the production designer of the previous two films, to go to America to do a third film with Oliver Stone.

He said, 'Don't get too excited as we are going to some downbeat areas of America, and will film in the notorious Statesville Correctional Centre at Joliet'. That's where some of the most violent people in the state of Illinois are incarcerated, sometimes for life. Out of the 1,500 prisoners at least 16 per cent are lifers for violent murder! The film, appropriately enough, was called *Natural Born Killers*.

Victor told me I should join them the following week to begin the first recce with Oliver and Bob Richardson, the lighting cameraman. We packed up the house and my kit, and within forty-eight hours we were winging our way over to America for another five months of work.

The recce was most memorable, as I was included in a very small team of six to support Oliver in his quest to nail down all the locations required for the script. Oliver was meticulous in the planning of each location, and on one occasion we visited an old, empty supermarket which we were going to use for Woody Harrelson to access some drugs he needed for the storyline. Oliver wanted it lit only with green tinted fluorescent lights and we found a pharmaceutical supplier to restock all the shelving with old bankrupt stock.

The supermarket frontage was all glass and, knowing from the script that the action with a pump shotgun was going to be a bit brutal, I asked Oliver which part of the glass frontage we should prepare for breakaway safety glass. I should have guessed the reply – 'All of it'. It was about 60ft wide. I knew then that this, as Mae West once said, was going to be a 'fun but bumpy ride'.

At all of the stops we made in New Mexico, especially out in the country, we were warned about rattlesnakes. I'm not sure where Bob Richardson found that old car fan belt from, but he took great delight in scaring the hell out of each of us in turn, when he thought we were off guard. We were featuring snakes a lot in the film, and they almost became a symbol of evil for our two characters (Micky & Mallory), who were on the run with no holds barred. The brutal scenes in a wayside diner, where all but one of the visiting customers are killed in cold blood, meant we had to build the whole thing as a set, because by the end of the scene, when Micky and Mallory leave, the whole place was wrecked. The lime green theme continued through the scene, so Key Lime Pie was the order of the day as I remember.

Finally, arriving back in Chicago, we were all invited to dine with Oliver who was having his first meeting

▲ Our lead actor, posing for a snap!

with Tommy Lee Jones. The snow started falling about an hour before the stretched limo came for us. Moving cautiously around the Chicago traffic, we arrived at a nice-looking restaurant where they had set up a table in a small annex with a red rope across the entrance. Tommy Lee Jones entertained us with a lot of funny stories, including some about working with Harrison Ford on *The Fugitive*, which he had just finished the week before. It was whilst we were in the grip of another anecdote that a young lady climbed over the red rope barrier and asked Tommy Lee Jones for his autograph. Tommy obliged and she thanked him and left, during which time Oliver stood up, and – tongue in cheek – said 'I'm famous too!' which of course he was, certainly just as famous as Tommy Lee Jones. However, the lady never looked back to see who she had missed!

On another dinner out in Chicago we were all on a big round table, and I was approached by a very attractive woman who leaned over to ask if I would appear on her evening chat show, of which she was the anchor woman. Knowing she had mistaken me for Oliver Stone, I asked what my appearance on her show would entail. Then, after a couple of minutes I dropped in the line, 'I could say what fun it is working on my third film with Oliver Stone?' Her face froze, she looked embarrassed and asked 'If you are not Oliver Stone, who is?' It just proved that your name can be famous but unless you are an actor on screen, your face does not get the same recognition!

On the final day of the recce we drove out to the Statesville correctional facility itself. This was where we were going to film a prison riot using dummy rubber weapons. We met the governor, and he said they would shortlist some inmates we could use as extras during the ten days' shooting within the prison.

Joliet was the last remaining round house. That is, a circular building with cells on four levels, all guarded by two prison guards with pump shotguns who walked around a central tower with a metal access door which had no handles at ground level. We were taken over to a long cell block of three levels, where the guards walked on the far side, mid-level, to cover all the cells on the far side. I was introduced to an old guy in a towelling robe by one of the guards, he reminded me a bit of Noel Coward in *The Italian Job*. After he left, I asked the guard what he was in prison for. 'Murdering his wife' he said, to which I replied 'I guess there are lots of prisoners in here for that'.

'Yes', he said, 'but most don't make use of a blender to get rid of the evidence'. I swallowed hard.

We had heard from the governor that, on a previous film shot in the prison, one of the prisoners had chatted up a third assistant female director and, wearing her crew jacket and her earphone and microphone set, calmly walked out and boarded the crew bus at the end of the day. That being the case, you can

imagine the security for us going in and coming out each day whilst we were shooting.

The film did very well, with Oliver being nominated for a Golden Globe Award, and top awards for Juliette Lewis at the Venice Film Festival.

I really enjoyed my trilogy with Oliver Stone, and whilst he was a hard taskmaster, he is undoubtedly one of the most brilliant directors in the business – and it shows on screen. ❏

19 *101 Dalmatians* (1995)

Our number one priority on this film was the interests and safety of all the little dogs. In fact, special deluxe kennels were built on the backlot at Shepperton and, with it being winter, they were all insulated and heated to the temperature recommended by the breeders. Each kennel floor was covered in a thick carpet and adorned with toys, and divided into pink and blue sections to keep the puppies happy. Such was their luxury that we were sure it wouldn't be long before TVs and video machines would be installed to entertain them when they were not required on set.

Although we never had all 101 puppies in one sitting, we did have to double up with further litters all the way through the shoot, as the leading pups grew a lot over the period of our months-long shooting schedule. Eight weeks old was the ideal age, but they were too old by the time they'd reached twelve weeks.

My first job was to make a cardboard scale model of the mansion belonging to our lead villain, Cruella de Vil (Glenn Close), to show the director how the interiors would all work. You see, for the puppies to climb the stairs we were told that they could not be more than 4in (10cm) high, and that made the baronial staircase very long to climb to reach the first floor level.

The exterior of the mansion was built in composite with the ground floor, first floor and roof. Assheton Gorton, our production designer, had all the brackets

FILM CREDITS

101 Dalmatians
(Supervising Art Director)
Director: Steve Herek
Stars: Glenn Close, Jeff Daniels

◀ A model of the main entrance to the de Vil mansion.

▲ The whole second unit crew.

➤ Another view of the model of the mansion, given some scale with a real live person in shot.

and corbels sculpted with spooky faces on each, and what with all the dark panelled walls the whole set took on a sort of haunted house effect.

The puppies' welfare was, as I mentioned, a top priority, since we all knew that if one died during the filming the press would have a field day and Disney, representing all things good in a child's eyes, would likely shut the project down. So, the love and affection shown to these puppies by twelve attractive kennel maids was top-notch; even some of the crew began to envy them. On one occasion on the huge H-stage, a lamp was put under some tinder-dry fir trees to create an effect and suddenly they ignited and burst into flames. The fire spread from the bottom to the top of the trees in seconds. The call went out 'THE PUPPIES, THE PUPPIES!', and as the trainers rushed around picking up the pups from the set, one electrician rushed by me saying, 'Sod the puppies, what about the humans?' Luckily the standby firemen were very quick on the ball and put out the burning trees.

The breeders accompanied their respective puppies to the studio daily, and the company met all their travel and accommodation costs whilst their dogs went through their ongoing training which had, in fact, started two weeks prior to them arriving at the studios. This 'pre-delivery' training at the breeders' houses also proved to us that the litters were healthy and there was no likelihood of them spreading anything onto the other pups when they met up.

Gary Gero, the head animal trainer, co-ordinated the whole of the programme like a military manoeuvre and no puppy stayed longer than four weeks at the studio, and one to two weeks was more common. I was told that the total number of puppies used over the whole film was closer to 201! John Freed, the representative from the America Humane Association, said 'These dogs were the healthiest and happiest I've ever seen on any film set, and I have seen a lot!'

Of course, continuity was all-important and so matching the spots on the dogs with vegetable dye to match the named characters was great fun, albeit a bit unusual for the make-up artist. But the puppies

◄◄ The actual set rebuilt in Florida Disneyland, forming part of their *101 Dalmatians* exhibition.

▲ In Florida, my production office was faithfully recreated – even my pin board was as I'd left it when we wrapped!

with the half-black tail, known in the film as 'Dip Stick' were the easiest to repeat.

The kitchen set where the Dalmatian mother dog 'Perdy' gives birth to her puppies, under the corner draining board with a draw curtain, was built twice – once in the studio, and again at a selected breeder's house. We constructed it early enough for the mother to get used to her new basket and private, screened 'delivery area'. The most difficult job was then for a camera crew to standby in close proximity to the house, and be ready to set up the required shots within a few minutes of 'Perdy' giving birth. We were all surprised, on seeing the rushes, that all the newborn puppies didn't have any spots. Little did we know that spots only arrive after about three weeks!

As a child I was always fascinated by car number plates, especially making names up with cunning arrangements, so I hit on the idea of giving Cruella de Vil's car a personalised plate. The car was adapted from an aptly named Panther De Ville, and we gave it a special black and ivory paint job. 'DEV-IL' was a regular number, but for obvious reasons it was not released for general use. This meant we had to get special permission from the DVLA (Driving and Vehicle Licensing Agency) to have the plates made up just for the film.

After the film was shown, Assheton and I were invited to Disneyland in Florida, to view the *101 Dalmatian* exhibition that had been built, which included some original sets from the film, including the exterior of Cruella's mansion. We'd had them cut up, and shipped over in containers at the end of shooting. The exhibition also had replicas of our offices, complete with drawing board and my large pin board which contained an assortment of notes and photos that had grown during the course of the film. I asked why everything on the pin board was reproduced.

▲ There's nothing like a bit of advertising, for the Florida exhibition.

➤ Glenn Close played our wonderful Cruella de Vil.

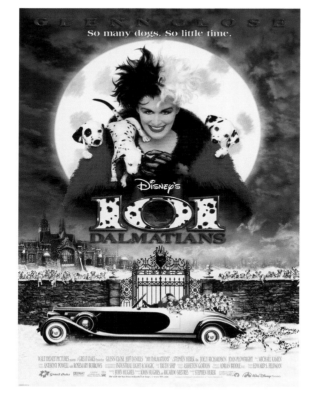

I was told that Disney kept all the originals, so that if any items are stolen, they can just print off another.

The Disney representative giving us the tour asked about the number plate and I was delighted to say I came up with the idea!

Working with animals is never easy – we had a host of them besides the dogs – and I was particularly impressed with how the animal trainers managed to keep all the farmyard beasts in the barn scenes, to do all their acting to order.

The UK premiere was held on 4 December at the Royal Albert Hall, and the whole of the exterior of the building was cleverly lit with black spots for the evening. Disney and its shareholders must have been pleased since it made $320 million worldwide at the box office. ❏

Saving Private Ryan **(1997)**

Saving Private Ryan is an American epic war film set during the invasion of Normandy in the Second World War, starring Tom Hanks and Matt Damon, and directed by Steven Spielberg. My main job on this movie was to source all the vehicles, tanks, planes and boats required.

The first thing I discovered was that no functioning Tiger tanks existed anywhere in England. The sole Tiger in 'captivity' was at the Bovington Tank Museum, but at that time was a non-runner. However, it was as authentic as you could get in order for us to photo-graph, take wheel moulds and build our own. In fact, we finished up making two. I recruited Steve Lamonby of Plus Films to construct them using the basic shell and motor of a T-34 Russian tank that had the same gun barrel height and overall sizes and would enable us to transform it into a Tiger.

My next big task was to build (or find) the landing craft for the beach invasion scenes. Health & Safety deemed it necessary to have the same standard of safety features as if we were sending twenty-five men across the Channel in them, and not just 100m off-

FILM CREDITS

Saving Private Ryan
Director: Steven Spielberg
Stars: Tom Hanks, Matt Damon
Received American Art Direction nomination

The invasion starts. A lot of this was achieved with a matte-shot.

shore, so the hunt was on for seaworthy landing craft. In the meantime, I had plans drawn up to build them, but, with the cost of £35,000 per boat my meagre departmental budget wasn't going to go very far.

Director Steven Spielberg, originally asked for twenty landing craft. However, I found out that he hadn't planned to film any air-to-ground shots, so I said it would be unlikely you would see more than ten in any one shot. He agreed, so I halved my problems!

Then our producer, Ian Bryce, heard from an American contact that twelve landing craft were available to purchase in Palm Springs. Believe it or not, with the added cost of shipping them over, they were still cheaper than I could make them for. They duly arrived at our location in Ireland, after being made seaworthy, with all safety equipment fitted by the Squaresail Company. They also gave them the correct Second World War finish with painting and signwriting.

⌃ A terrific shot of a landing craft beaching itself after hitting a mine.

➤ Tom Hanks and Matt Damon pose in our street set.

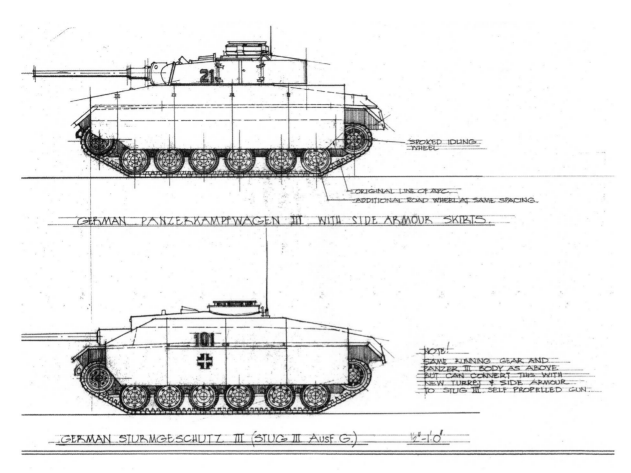

SPOKED IDLING
WHEEL

ORIGINAL LINE OF APC.
ADDITIONAL ROAD WHEEL AT SAME SPACING.

GERMAN PANZERKAMPFWAGEN III WITH SIDE ARMOUR SKIRTS.

NOTE!
SAME RUNNING GEAR AND
PANZER III BODY AS ABOVE
BUT CAN CONVERT THIS WITH
NEW TURRET & SIDE ARMOUR
TO STUG III SELF PROPELLED GUN.

GERMAN STURMGESCHUTZ III (STUG III AusF G.)   ½"-1'0'

◀ Two of my drawings outlining ideas to convert purchased army APCs into German tanks.

Throughout the preparation period of the film, we only had one conference call to Spielberg, as he was busy in LA cutting his last film. He had a great trust in us all to deliver the main D-Day Landings beach set, which we finally did after much hunting for a location in Ireland.

Spielberg was due to arrive three days before shooting started, and I was asked to fly back to London, as he wanted to tour our Hatfield location base and had expressly asked to see the Tiger tanks we were building. I stayed in my own house that night,

and had the strange experience of ringing my wife whilst she was on the location in Ireland, instead of the other way around.

The next day we all met up with Spielberg at the Hatfield base to show him our two Tiger tanks, and he remarked how much smaller they were than he had imagined. I knew they were built to the exact sizes from the measurements I took from the real tank in Bovington, plus the plans and elevations we had sourced prior to obtaining the two T-34s to alter. I did say to Spielberg that, when drawn in comics, they

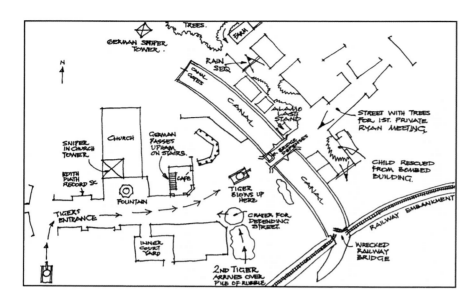

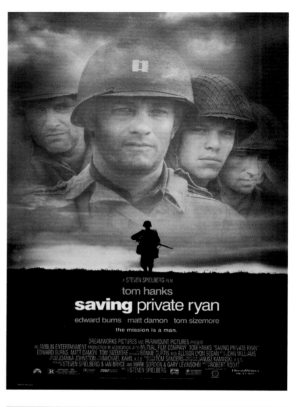

▲ My sketch plan showing the layout, and where the various action sequences were filmed.

➤ Tom Hanks and Matt Damon.

➤➤ The twelve GMCs which I sourced in order to make our convoy scenes look busy.

always made them more menacing by making them a percentage larger than life-size. He seemed happy.

The next day, we all travelled back to Ireland to show him the landing location which would represent Omaha Beach in Normandy. Spielberg loved it, and told Tom Sanders, our production designer so. Having walked the beach area, it was impossible for the special effects team to put all their explosive require-

ments in place for the next morning, but Spielberg wanted to get started and get to know everyone, so he very cleverly wrote an extra scene of our heroes confronting a German convoy on the road. Sadly, although we put out six of our best German vehicles

◄ A high-angle shot of our recreated street set, taken from the church tower.

in the convoy, it was edited out of the finished film. The most memorable thing from that first day was that the location was close to a very small village called Screen – how apt for Hollywood's top director to begin his D-Day epic in Screen.

My favourite German vehicle was a half-track motorbike called a *'Kettenkrad'*. Being a tracked vehicle it could go over any terrain, including ploughed fields, so I had the idea that we could get the Americans to use an abandoned one to lure the Tiger tanks into town for our final scenes. I put the idea to our technical advisor, Dale Dye, a long-time friend of mine from working on *JFK*. He thought it was a good idea and said he would run it by Spielberg at the next opportunity. So, the idea of using the *Kettenkrad* as

the 'rabbit' was born. I never did worry if Spielberg knew it was my idea, as long as it benefits the film and the director is happy that is basically my remit on any film.

Before the end of shooting I wanted to take all the vehicles we had purchased, plus the ones on hire, and make a line-up on the historic runway (from which the first jet passenger plane, the Comet, took off). I had to choose a day where we could use all of our driver-mechanics to ferry them out, and then use a Jeep to bring the drivers back to collect another four vehicles. It also had to be a day when our department had nothing on set. Our excellent standby mechanic, Peter Tombs, set them up as they arrived at the runway. ❏

21 *Batman Begins* (2005)

FILM CREDITS

Batman Begins
Director: Christopher Nolan
Stars: Christian Bale,
Michael Caine

Although there had been a 'reboot' of Batman for the big screen in 1989 (with Tim Burton at the helm), and into the early 1990s, with everyone from Michael Keaton to George Clooney donning the cape, I was intrigued to hear that British director, Christopher Nolan, was going to breathe new life into the franchise in 2005.

I was even more intrigued when I was asked to join the new film, to take on the complex ideas that the director and his American production designer, Nathan Crowley, had come up with for the new Batmobile. In fact, Nathan had worked so closely with

Christopher on the designs for both the Batmobile and the enormous streets of Gotham City that he had built a huge model in Christopher's garage in Los Angeles.

When they both travelled to England, the crated model arrived soon after! They also brought over a small model of the 'unusual elements' that they wanted to feature in the Batmobile, such as six massive tyres doubled up on the rear and the front steering wheels, driven and steered from outside, thus eliminating a front axle. I thought this was going to be a real challenge for the special effects engineers.

➤ The original camouflage pattern of the Batmobile.

With all the rest of the art department working on the many hundreds of detailed working drawings required to build the streets of Gotham City and all the other sets, I started to push the ideas for the Batmobile into shape, first in drawings and then as a plasticard model. It sounds like I had an easy job, but in fact any prop – or film set – has to be built from tens if not hundreds of drawings, and so it can take many weeks just to come up with one element of the movie. Talk about intensive!

Naturally, security on a film such as this, which has a huge amount of hype and expectation attached, is always tight. So much so, I was asked to hide the model and cover my drawing board with a dust sheet every night in case the cleaners saw it. Mind you, if you ever saw the night cleaning lady who looked after our block of offices, I'm sure you'd agree she would not know the difference between a Batmobile and a mobile home. This strict security thing – which is now commonplace on all films – was new to me, but like good soldiers we obeyed the orders without quibble.

I very quickly realised that Christopher and Nathan were making the Batmobile their number one design, so almost every day I'd get a visit from our director. Thankfully, he always came with Nathan and they evaluated every aspect between them, with lots of discussions, such as 'how Batman would enter the vehicle'. The design went from gull-wing door openings to hydraulic opening roof and windscreen, like a jet fighter. Keeping up with all the changes was very demanding, and with time ticking by I was under huge pressure to deliver a set of drawings that could be issued to the construction department.

Nathan had a great idea to make a full-size replica in polystyrene, but still using the big wheels that special effects had sourced from America. This full-size polystyrene Batmobile was fashioned into shape

by a sculptor, and on completion we painted the whole thing matt black.

Having lived with the project for three months through so many ideas and changes, the day finally came to show it to Christopher for a final nod of approval. He duly arrived with Nathan, and I let them know how pleased I was with the final concept and sizes, which came in at 15ft 2in long and 9ft 2in wide, but only 5ft in height.

For something so stylish and futuristic, it had such an unglamorous birth – black-painted polystyrene, carved in a Second World War Nissen hut without any form of heating and a very leaky roof. I thought it reminiscent of a baby being born in a stable-type hut. Well, it was near Christmas!

Anyhow, Nathan and Christopher arrived and walked around it many times. 'What more could they change?' I wondered. Then Christopher said he thought it should be one and a half inches lower. I could not help saying, 'don't worry, we'll let the tyres down a bit'. I thought it might amuse him, but it went down like a lead balloon, or in this case, a flat tyre.

Once any working drawings, details, and full-size panel layouts leave your office and go to the special

▼ And here it is again in matt black.

▲▲ Director Christopher Nolan chats through a sequence with Katie Holmes.

▲ Christopher Nolan with stars, Christian Bale and Michael Caine.

The first prototype went out to a vehicle proving ground under much security, and stunt driver George Cottle was the lucky guy to put it through its paces. To his delight, and ours, it could do everything that was asked of it. This was still two weeks before the start of filming, so for once we were ahead of the game. At this point a second Batmobile was started – you always need a spare on a movie like this.

To see the 'Tumbler' (the scripted name for the Batmobile) going into a sideways spin on the test track was proof enough that the special effects engineers had fulfilled Christopher's objective, that it would 'perform like a two and a half ton sports car'. I think it was Nathan who said it was a cross between a Ferrari and a Hummer.

For continued security, a 10ft high, walled room was made within one of the stages, and under the cover of darkness the polystyrene Batmobile was transferred from the Nissen hut to the stage. The entrance door was padlocked and I held the key. I was often asked to escort guests of the director and his wife (who was one of the producers) to the 'Batmobile garage'. On one of my trips to show a guest around, we got to talking about the year's best performances. You see, I've been a member of the American Academy (Oscars) since 2003, and have the opportunity to vote for the awards. Anyhow, I mentioned that I felt Tom Cruise's portrayal of Nathan Algren in *The Last Samurai* was one of his best performances, and I was amazed it was not even nominated. The guest looked me square in the eyes and said, 'That's wonderful, because I'm his agent'. What's the chance of that happening?

In all, six Batmobiles were built. The first two were street-driving versions, another one was built with more hydraulic enhancements for moving rear brake flaps, doors etc., and there was one specially adapted

effects department, it becomes their baby. As a surrogate father I did have visiting rights in the early days whilst the prototype was being constructed, and was delighted that the engineers on the team did such a fantastic job.

∧ Liam Neeson played Ra's al Ghul, head of the League of Shadows organisation.

➤ Gary Oldman and Christian Bale are on location atop a Chicago skyscraper.

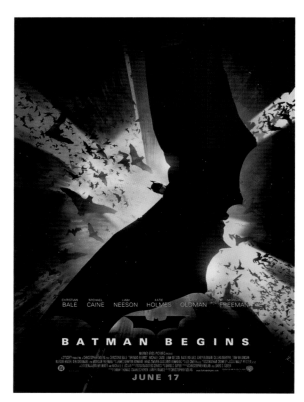

to contain vast propane tanks that would fuel the rear blast of the fired rocket engine when seen going away from camera.

I was very satisfied with my final working drawing, and knew from the Snowspeeder drawing I'd made for *Star Wars* that there'd likely be thousands of plastic kits produced from them when the film was released.

Oh! And another satisfying job I had on the film was to come up with an army camouflage design for when Batman first confronts the vehicle in the army storage facility. I produced four different ideas, and I had learnt from a past master to always keep the best for last. I felt that the best was the very angular shapes based on the German 'splinter' camouflage, which is dark grey on white ground. This was applied to their tanks and trucks to make them less visible in snowy conditions. Since most of the world's conflicts are fought in the desert, I did all the four configurations in ginger brown over a sand background, the standard colours for desert warfare. I even gave a nod to the Second World War camouflage pattern known as 'Mickey Mouse' camo, since its shape often looked like Mickey's ears.

So, playing the proverbial 'four-card trick', the agreed camouflage pattern was the desert splinter design. When the film was released, it was nice to see a Mattel 'Hotwheels' version sporting the desert splinter camouflage (see photo on p. 146).

I felt somewhat disappointed when a team of special effects engineers toured all the major European cities' premieres exhibiting the Batmobile, and not once did Nathan, our designer, receive an invitation. Nor, from the publicity I read, was he hardly ever mentioned. It's a bit like forgetting the architect and praising the builders.

More recently, I felt a great sense of pride when watching a TV news item about the Duke and Duchess of Cambridge visiting the new Warner Brothers Studio in Leavesden. The duke was taken to see the Batmobile and his face beamed as he approached it – a look only bettered later in the year when he emerged from the hospital with his newborn son, Prince George. ❏

22 *Casino Royale* (2005)

After working on any successful franchise film you always wonder if your input earned you enough points to be asked back, so when Peter Lamont asked me to join him on 007's twenty-first outing I was flattered. *Casino Royale* was to be my sixth, with my fourth actor playing Bond. It really is like being part of a big family that you visit every couple of years and stay with for a few months. That feeling only pervades through the leadership of Barbara Broccoli and Michael G. Wilson, who have run the franchise since their father, Cubby Broccoli, handed the reigns over to them on his death.

I'd already worked two years past retirement age, and with the government giving me the weekly state pension in one hand and the tax man taking it away with the other, I thought it was about time I considered retiring and enjoying some of the fruits of my labour! Since *Dr No* was my first Bond film in 1961, it seemed only fitting that this was a perfect film on which to complete my fifty years in the business and hang up my T-square.

Production designer Peter Lamont knew my wife was from Rome, and that Venice was the city of her father. In fact, one of the palaces on the Grand Canal is named 'Pesaro Palace' (which is the family name), so I can only surmise that way back in the family tree, the noble and wealthy Pesaro family had the

FILM CREDITS

Casino Royale
Director: Martin Campbell
Stars: Daniel Craig, Eva Green

◄ The Bond art department on *Die Another Day*, many of whom joined me for *Casino Royale* when we shipped out to studios in Prague.

⌃ The models I made of the 'sinking house' set in Venice.

baroque palace built. From 1710 until 1830 it stayed in the Pesaro family and then with mounting debts it was given to the city of Venice to establish a new art gallery.

Having visited Venice many times to see my wife's friends, I had amassed a lot of great reference books about various palaces along the waterfronts and after taking them all into the office, Peter asked me to look after the massive interior set of the sinking palace. I was surprised that the script called for a four-storey building to sink into the canal, because on our many visits to Venice I had seen sections of the canals drained to facilitate repairs to the foundations, and these areas are mostly around 5m deep (that is to say about one storey high, not four). Peter advised me not

to worry as the majority of the cinema public will 'just enjoy the action as it happens'.

After I had designed a plan and elevations of the interior, Peter asked me to make a model of the four storey set to enable our director to work out his action. Having completed one model, we had to make a large wooden crate to ship it out for meetings and discussions in Venice. Various other departments, including special effects, really needed a repeat model for their discussions in London, so off I went again and built another model, but this time with some help from other members of the art department.

The whole set was to be constructed on the 007 Stage at Pinewood, and built into a vast hydraulic metal rig that would move the set down into a tank of

◄ Daniel Craig, looking very intense in a scene with Venice in the background.

◄◄ Daniel Craig sampling his Vesper Martini, with Eva Green.

water. The whole rig weighed in at 80 tons, and it was the largest ever built for a film. It was all controlled from a bank of computers and a massive keyboard. The water tank under the set was increased to a depth of 19ft (5.8m) to achieve the 'amount of sinking depth' required. This meant the set was built right up to the grid of the roof of the huge stage!

To celebrate my half-century in the business, I arranged a bit of a celebration lunch. People called in all over lunchtime for a glass of wine and some lovely snacks. I invited our executive producer, Anthony Waye, who arrived with his first letter of employment, which beat mine by a few months. He had started as a post-boy at Pinewood early in 1955.

Another nice reunion was with the English editor Stuart Baird, who I first worked with on *The Devils* in 1971, when Stuart was promoted to assistant editor. I had not seen him for years, as he spent most of his editing time in America where he specialised in action

➤ The Aston Martin completed seven full rolls, earning the stunt a place in the *Guinness Book of Records.*

▼ Very 'Bondian'. The DB5 on location in the Bahamas.

movies and also directed a few big films. It was a good move to get Stuart over.

Casino Royale was a terrific film to finish on, as it received the 'Excellence in Production Design' award from the American Art Directors Guild, as well as numerous BAFTA nominations. Oh, and another memorable award was given out at the crew show in London on 5 November 2006. The Aston Martin in which Bond swerves to avoid Vesper (Eva Green) laying in the road, was going very fast indeed and was driven by stunt driver Adam Kiley. It was fitted with a nitrogen ram to help it flip over and roll. In fact, it rolled over seven times, which was a new record, and Andy went on stage to collect his *Guinness Book of Records* framed diploma to the cheers of the film crew.

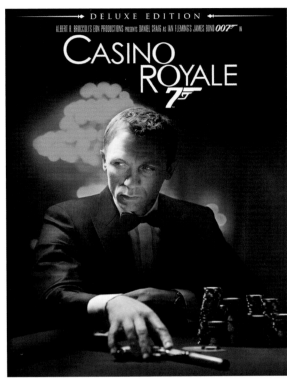

▲ The large-scale model of the exterior of the sinking house, built on the paddock tank at Pinewood. The centre section was on hydraulics.

◄◄ The Art Directors' Guild nominated us for a design award – which we went on to win.

◄ The interior of the sinking house, with Eva Green as Vesper trapped inside the lift.

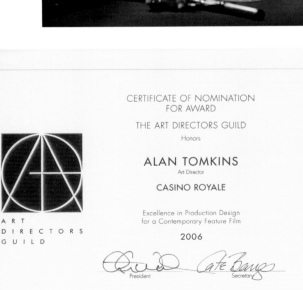

CERTIFICATE OF NOMINATION
FOR AWARD

THE ART DIRECTORS GUILD
Honors

ALAN TOMKINS
Art Director

CASINO ROYALE

Excellence in Production Design
for a Contemporary Feature Film

2006

President   Secretary

ART
DIRECTORS
GUILD

The film went on to become the highest grossing Bond film, only to be beaten by *Skyfall* in November 2012. So I guess you could say I went out on a high – it's certainly nice to cap fifty years in the industry on a successful film, that's for sure. ❏

23 In Closing

I've always considered getting my start in the business as being down to sheer unadulterated luck, and I was very lucky to have such brilliant teachers during my three year apprenticeship, that's for sure. (Though I did discover later on that I do actually have a family connection with cinema 'royalty', whom I might have called on for a leg up. My father set out our family tree, and showed me how we were related, albeit by marriage, to the Chaplin family – Charlie being their most famous son! But I didn't find that out until years after I'd started.)

The half-century I spent in the art department was undoubtedly among the most exciting time in the whole history of the film business. Not only was I working with some of the best designers, but the industry was evolving and developed at such pace. I suppose we were really – unknowingly – the archi-

tects of the astonishing developments that have followed since.

At the start of my career, for instance, everything had to be done 'for real' in front of the camera, but with the digital technology revolution many of the toughest and seemingly impossible sequences and sets could be achieved via CGI magic. The production designers no longer had to say 'sorry it can't be done' to their directors, and instead had a chat with colleagues in the effects and post-production departments to make everything (and anything) possible.

Whilst blowing my trumpet for the designers, I'm also very conscious of the contribution made by the craftsmen – carpenters, painters and plasters etc. –

▼ My certificate of acceptance to membership of the Academy of Motion Picture Arts and Sciences (or the Oscars, if you like).

➤ I was proud and delighted to be Emmy nominated for my work on *Gulliver's Travels*.

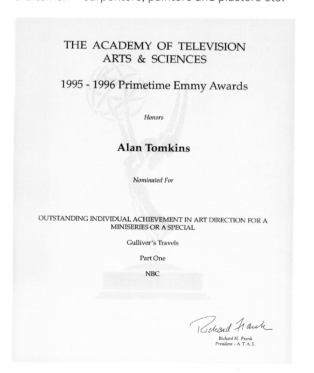

HAVING DEMONSTRATED EXCEPTIONAL

ACCOMPLISHMENTS IN THE FIELD OF

THEATRICAL MOTION PICTURES,

Alan R. Tomkins

HAS BEEN ACCEPTED AS A MEMBER OF THE

President

ACADEMY OF MOTION PICTURE ARTS AND SCIENCES

THE ACADEMY OF TELEVISION
ARTS & SCIENCES

1995 - 1996 Primetime Emmy Awards

Honors

Alan Tomkins

Nominated For

OUTSTANDING INDIVIDUAL ACHIEVEMENT IN ART DIRECTION FOR A
MINISERIES OR A SPECIAL

Gulliver's Travels

Part One

NBC

Richard H. Frank
President - A.T.A.S.

London, November 14, 1990

Dear Sir,

I am very happy to have the opportunity to sponsor Alan Tomkins for an H-I permit enabling him to work in America.

He was my Art Director on ''HAMLET'' which we shot earlier this year and I know with his talent he will be an asset to the industry there.

Regards, *and thanks*

Franco Zeffirelli

Franco Zeffirelli

Dear Al
Thank you for
helping so wholeheartedly.
You are Truly a prince.

Gene

who are so often forgotten. Yet, without them, all the drawings in the world would amount to nothing. In the UK we have some of the most talented craftsmen in the world, and I think I am a good judge, having constructed sets in America, Canada, Mexico and ten European countries. I salute them all.

Every job has its high and lows, but the highs have far outweighed everything for me. Seeing my modest contributions to the overall design of a film never failed to excite me and spur me on, but when I received the totally unexpected news that I'd been nominated for an Oscar on *The Empire Strikes Back* at the 53rd Academy Awards, it became the icing on a very big cake.

⌃ Franco Zeffirelli kindly offered to write a letter of sponsorship helping enable me to work in the US.

◂◂ A treasured note of praise from Gene Wilder.

◂ The role of an art director – three photos showing how we can add to an existing location to achieve another look. *Interview with the Vampire*, in New Orleans.

➤ With my supportive wife, Titti, when I won the Emmy.

➤➤ In Normandy I'm only known as 'Father T', after this small part I was asked to play in *Band of Brothers*, episode 4.

Once we'd landed in LA, my wife and I devoted the whole day of the Oscars to relaxing and preparing for the 4.30 p.m. pick-up to whisk us off to the Dorothy Chandler Pavilion for our walk down that famous long red carpet, surrounded by hundreds of the world's press. At about 3 p.m., and already in my tuxedo, we heard that the whole event was put on hold as someone in Washington had taken a shot at President Reagan and he'd been rushed to the hospital. As it was only hours before the live, televised event, we knew we wouldn't be going anywhere. However, the president was aware of the Oscars being cancelled and insisted that the ceremony should go ahead the next day. I thought about the poor chefs who'd been preparing the four course dinner for 500 people at the Governor's Ball honouring all the nominees that evening, only to be told at that eleventh hour to hold everything and start again tomorrow.

Anyhow, we repeated our timetable the next day, and duly arrived down in the lobby of our hotel for the 4.30 p.m. pick-up. 'Car for Alan Tomkins' came the call over the speaker system. We went out but could only see a white stretched limo waiting under the canopy. I knew Dolly Parton was also staying there, as she was nominated for her song '9 to 5', so I went back into the lobby to say I could only see a limo outside for Miss Parton and asked where I should go to find my car. They said that *was* my car! That was just the start of a very memorable evening.

◄ With Franco Zeffirelli whilst working on *Hamlet*.

My good friend Jack Stevens won in our category, for Roman Polanski's *Tess*, and as we were all on the same big table for dinner afterwards we had his Oscar for our table centrepiece for the evening!

Amongst the many other highs of my career was meeting so many of the real heroes of the Second World War films I worked on. Some are still acquaintances, after these many years, especially the guys who formed the American spearhead, parachuting into Normandy on 6 June 1944.

However, without doubt the biggest and proudest memory I have was being asked by John Huston to direct Paul Newman in *The Mackintosh Man*. I still pinch myself.

So, when youngsters ask me for some worldly advice about the art department nowadays, I always tell them, 'If a bit of luck comes your way, grab it, work hard and the rewards of a job well done are excessive'. I also tell them what my grandmother once said to me, 'You get no second chance to make a first impression'.

I'm proud to have been a part of this magical and amazing business and I hope you've enjoyed sharing a few of my adventures. ❏

Filmography

As Art Director (unless otherwise indicated):

2005 ***Casino Royale***
Director: Martin Campbell
Stars: Daniel Craig, Eva Green

2003 ***Batman Begins***
Director: Christopher Nolan
Stars: Christian Bale, Michael Caine

2002 ***Tomb Raider II***
Director: Jan de Bont
Stars: Angelina Jolie, Gerard Butler

2002 ***Die Another Day***
Director: Lee Tamahori
Stars: Pierce Brosnan, Halle Berry

2001 ***Reign of Fire***
Director: Rob Bowman
Stars: Christian Bale, Matthew McConaughey

2000 ***Band of Brothers*** (Supervising Art Director)
Director: Various
Stars: Scott Grimes, Damian Lewis

1999 ***Don Quixote*** (Supervising Art Director)
Director: Peter Yates
Stars: John Lithgow, Bob Hoskins

1999 ***A Christmas Carol*** (Supervising Art Director)
Director: David Jones
Stars: Patrick Stewart, Richard E. Grant

1998 **Alice in Wonderland** (Supervising Art Director)
Director: Nick Willing
Stars: Tina Majorino, Whoopi Goldberg
Received Emmy nomination for Art Direction

1997 ***Saving Private Ryan***
Director: Steven Spielberg
Stars: Tom Hanks, Matt Damon
Received American Art Direction nomination

1996 ***Kundun*** (Supervising Art Director)
Director: Martin Scorsese
Stars: Tenzin Thuthob Tsarong, Gyurme Tethong
Received Academy Award nomination for Art Direction

1995 ***101 Dalmatians*** (Supervising Art Director)
Director: Steve Herek
Stars: Glenn Close, Jeff Daniels

**** ***Gulliver's Travels***
Director: Charles Sturridge
Stars: Ted Danson, Mary Steenburgen
Won Emmy award

1994 ***Rob Roy***
Director: Michael Caton-Jones
Stars: Liam Neeson, Jessica Lange

1993 **Interview with the Vampire** (Supervising Art Director – USA)
Director: Neil Jordan
Stars: Tom Cruise, Brad Pitt

Natural Born Killers (Supervising Art Director)
Director: Oliver Stone
Stars: Woody Harrelson, Juliette Lewis

1993 **Heaven & Earth** (Supervisor Art Director)
Director: Oliver Stone
Stars: Takaaki Enoki, Masahiko Tsugawa

1991 **JFK**
Director: Oliver Stone
Stars: Kevin Costner, Gary Oldman

1990 **Robin Hood: Prince of Thieves** (Supervising Art Director)
Director: Kevin Reynolds
Stars: Kevin Costner, Alan Rickman

Hamlet
Director: Franco Zeffirelli
Stars: Mel Gibson, Glenn Close

Women & Men: Stories of Seduction (Dusk before Fireworks and The Man in the Brooks Brother's Suit Segments)
Director: Ken Russell, Frederick Raphael
Stars: Beau Bridges, Melanie Griffith
Received Ace Award Nomination

1989 **Memphis Belle**
Director: Michael Caton-Jones
Stars: Mathew Modine, Eric Stoltz

1988–89 **Ticket to Ride/A Fine Romance** (Set Decorator)
Director: Various
Stars: Margaret Whitton, Ernie Sabella

1988 **Batman** (Assistant Art Director)
Director: Tim Burton
Stars: Michael Keaton, Jack Nicholson

A Dry White Season
Director: Euzhan Palcy
Stars: Donald Sutherland, Janet Suzman, Marlon Brando

1986 **High Spirits**
Director: Neil Jordan
Stars: Peter O'Toole, Daryl Hannah

Nostromo (Preparation only – project abandoned)
Director: David Lean
Stars: N/A

War & Remembrance
Director: Dan Curtis
Stars: Jane Seymour, Robert Mitchum

King Kong Lives (Assistant Art Director)
Director: John Guillermin
Stars: Brian Kerwin, Linda Hamilton

1985 **Haunted Honeymoon** (Supervising Art Director)
Director: Gene Wilder
Stars: Gene Wilder, Gilda Radner

Revolution (Assistant Art Director)
Director: Hugh Hudson
Stars: Al Pacino, Donald Sutherland

1984 **National Lampoon's European Vacation**
Director: Amy Heckerling
Stars: Chevy Chase, Beverly D'Angelo

A View to a Kill (Assistant Art Director)
Director: John Glen
Stars: Roger Moore, Tanya Roberts,
Christopher Walken

1983 **Space Vampires (aka Lifeforce)**
Director: Tobe Hooper
Stars: Steve Railsback, Mathilda May

Terry & the Pirates (Preparation only, in
Hong Kong. Film cancelled)
Director: Lewis Gilbert
Stars: Sean Connery, Michael Caine

Lassiter
Director: Roger Young
Stars: Tom Selleck, Jane Seymour

1982 **The Keep**
Director: Michael Mann
Stars: Scott Glenn, Ian McKellen

1981 **Trail of the Pink Panther** and **The Curse of
the Pink Panther**
Director: Blake Edwards
Stars: Peter Sellers, David Niven

Firefox
Director: Clint Eastwood
Stars: Clint Eastwood, Freddie Jones

1980 **Victor Victoria**
Director: Blake Edwards
Stars: Julie Andrews, James Garner

For Your Eyes Only (Assistant Art Director)
Director: John Glen
Stars: Roger Moore, Carole Bouquet

1979 **Green Ice**
Director: Ernest Day
Stars: Ryan O'Neal, Anne Archer, Omar
Sharif

1978 **Star Wars: The Empire Strikes Back**
Director: Irvin Kershner
Stars: Mark Hamill, Harrison Ford, Carrie
Fisher
Received Academy Award nomination

1977 **Hanover Street**
Director: Peter Hyams
Stars: Harrison Ford, Lesley-Anne Down,
Christopher Plummer

Love and Bullets
Director: Stuart Rosenberg
Stars: Charles Bronson, Jill Ireland

1976 **A Bridge Too Far**
Director: Richard Attenborough
Stars: Sean Connery, Ryan O'Neal, Michael
Caine, Dirk Bogarde

1975 **The Adventure of Sherlock Holmes'
Smarter Brother**
Director: Gene Wilder
Stars: Gene Wilder, Madeline Kahn

1974 **Royal Flash**
Director: Richard Lester
Stars: Malcolm McDowell, Alan Bates

Great Expectations
Director: Joseph Hardy
Stars: Michael York, Sarah Miles, James
Mason

Juggernaut
Director: Richard Lester
Stars: Richard Harris, Omar Sharif

1973 **The Mackintosh Man**
Director: John Huston
Stars: Paul Newman

The Glass Menagerie
Director: Tony Harvey
Stars: Katharine Hepburn, Sam Waterston,
Joanna Miles

The Abdication
Director: Tony Harvey
Stars: Peter Finch, Liv Ullmann

1972 **A Touch of Class**
Director: Melvin Frank
Stars: George Segal, Glenda Jackson

1971 **Mary, Queen of Scots** (Assistant Art
Director)
Director: Charles Jarrott
Stars: Vanessa Redgrave, Glenda Jackson,
Patrick McGoohan

The Public Eye (aka **Follow Me**)
Director: Carol Reed
Stars: Mia Farrow, Topol

1970 **The Tragedy of Macbeth** (Assistant Art
Director)
Director: Roman Polanski
Stars: Jon Finch, Francesca Annis, Martin
Shaw

The Devils
Director: Ken Russell
Stars: Vanessa Redgrave, Oliver Reed

The Challengers
Director: Leslie H. Martinson
Stars: Darren McGavin, Sean Garrison, Juliet
Mills

1969 **The Ballad of Tam Lin** (Assistant Art
Director)
Director: Roddy McDowell
Stars: Ava Gardner, Ian McShane

1968 **The Walking Stick** (Assistant Art Director)
Director: Eric Till
Stars: David Hemmings, Samantha Eggar,
Emlyn Williams

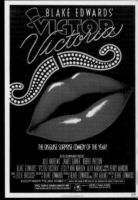

The Crusaders (Preparation only – film cancelled)
Director: Michael Winner

Attack on the Iron Coast
Director: Paul Wendkos
Stars: Lloyd Bridges, Andrew Keir, Sue Lloyd

Battle of Britain
Director: Guy Hamilton
Stars: Michael Caine, Trevor Howard

2001: A Space Odyssey
Director: Stanley Kubrick
Stars: Keir Dullea, Gary Lockwood, William Sylvester

1966 **Mr Ten Per Cent**
Director: Peter Graham Scott
Stars: Charlie Drake, Derek Nimmo, Wanda Ventham

1965 **The Baron** (Assistant Art Director)
Director: Various (thirty episodes)
Stars: Steve Forrest, Sue Lloyd, Paul Ferris

The Nanny
Director: Seth Holt
Stars: Bette Davies, Wendy Craig, Jill Bennett

1964 **The Heroes of Telemark** (Assistant Art Director)
Director: Anthony Mann
Stars: Kirk Douglas, Richard Harris, Ulla Jacobsson

The High Bright Sun (aka *McGuire, Go Home!*)
Director: Ralph Thomas
Stars: Dirk Bogarde, George Chakiris, Susan Strasberg

Lord Jim (Draughtsman)
Director: Richard Brooks
Stars: Peter O'Toole, James Mason, Curd Jürgens

1963 **The Moon-Spinners** (Assistant Art Director)
Director: James Neilson
Stars: Hayley Mills, Eli Wallach, Pola Negri

From Russia with Love (Assistant Art Director)
Director: Terence Young
Stars: Sean Connery, Robert Shaw, Lotte Lenya

1962 **Call Me Bwana** (Assistant Art Director)
Director: Gordon Douglas
Stars: Bob Hope, Anita Ekberg, Edie Adams

Summer Holiday
Director: Peter Yates
Stars: Cliff Richard, Lauri Peters, Melvyn Hayes

We Joined the Navy
Director: Wendy Toye
Stars: Kenneth More, Lloyd Nolan, Joan O'Brien

1961 **Dr No** (Assistant Art Director)
Director: Terence Young
Stars: Sean Connery, Ursula Andress,
Bernard Lee

Light in the Piazza (Draughtsman)
Director: Guy Green
Stars: Olivia de Havilland, George Hamilton,
Yvette Mimieux

Cleopatra (Draughtsman)
Director: Joseph Mankiewicz
Stars: Elizabeth Taylor, Richard Burton

Lawrence of Arabia (Draughtsman)
Director: David Lean
Stars: Peter O'Toole, Alec Guinness, Omar
Sharif

I worked on the following films whilst serving my
three year apprenticeship as a draftsman and
trainee assistant art director, plus those films for
a few years afterwards when I was contracted as
'staff' at ABPC studios, until I left to go freelance
in 1961:

1961 **The Rebel (aka Call Me Genius)**
Director: Robert Day
Stars: Tony Hancock, George Sanders

1960 **The Long, the Short and the Tall**
Director: Lindsay Anderson
Stars: Robert Shaw, Edward Judd

The Trials of Oscar Wilde
Director: Ken Hughes
Stars: Peter Finch, Yvonne Mitchell

Sands of the Desert
Director: John Paddy Carstairs
Stars: Charlie Drake, Peter Arne, Sarah Branch

The Roman Spring of Mrs Stone
Director: José Quintero
Stars: Vivien Leigh, Warren Beatty

Don't Bother to Knock
Director: Cyril Frankel
Stars: Richard Todd, Nicole Maurey, Elke
Sommer

1959 **Tommy the Toreador**
Director: John Paddy Carstairs
Stars: Tommy Steele, Janet Munro, Sidney
James

Look Back in Anger
Director: Tony Richardson
Stars: Richard Burton, Claire Bloom, Mary
Ure

The Sundowners
Director: Fred Zinnemann
Stars: Deborah Kerr, Robert Mitchum, Peter
Ustinov

1958 **Ice Cold in Alex**
Director: J. Lee Thompson
Stars: John Mills, Anthony Quayle, Sylvia
Syms

No Trees in the Street
Director: J. Lee Thompson
Stars: Sylvia Syms, Herbert Lom, Melvyn
Hayes

The Lady is a Square
Director: Herbert Wilcox
Stars: Anna Neagle, Frankie Vaughan, Janette Scott

Girls at Sea
Director: Gilbert Gunn
Stars: Guy Rolfe, Ronald Shiner, Michael Hordern

Alive and Kicking
Director: Cyril Frankel
Stars: Sybil Thorndike, Kathleen Harrison, Estelle Winwood

1957 **Woman in a Dressing Gown**
Director: J. Lee Thompson
Stars: Yvonne Mitchell, Anthony Quayle, Sylvia Syms

Night of the Demon (aka *Curse of the Demon*)
Director: Jacques Tourneur
Stars: Dana Andrews, Peggy Cummins, Niall MacGinnis

The Good Companions
Director: J. Lee Thompson
Stars: Eric Portman, Celia Johnson, Hugh Griffith

Chase a Crooked Shadow
Director: Michael Anderson
Stars: Richard Todd, Anne Baxter

The Moonraker
Director: David MacDonald
Stars: George Baker, Sylvia Syms, Marius Goring

Indiscreet
Director: Stanley Donen
Stars: Cary Grant, Ingrid Bergman, Cecil Parker

1956 **My Wife's Family**
Director: Gilbert Gunn
Stars: Ronald Shiner, Ted Ray, Greta Gynt

Let's Be Happy
Director: Henry Levin
Stars: Vera-Ellen, Tony Martin, Robert Flemyng

Interpol (aka *Pickup Alley*)
Director: John Gilling
Stars: Victor Mature, Anita Ekberg, Trevor Howard

1955 **Yield to the Night (aka *Blonde Sinner*)**
Director: J. Lee Thompson
Stars: Diana Dors, Yvonne Mitchell, Michael Craig

Acknowledgements

In writing this book I am indebted to the following individuals:

First and foremost, Gareth Owen who, despite not knowing the full details of all my film history at the beginning, still wanted to take my 'tinkerings' (as he called my notes) and mould them into this book.

Britt Ekland and Sally Geeson, whom I entertained with my tales at a film memorabilia dinner in November 2012. Both said I should write them all in a book, and added 'especially for your grandchildren and great grandchildren to read'. I thank them both for encouraging me enough to start writing soon after.

Oliver Stone, for writing such nice words of introduction. I never knew he liked me that much!

Our proofreader, Iris Harwood, who was so helpful in getting my grammar shipshape.

Barbara Broccoli and Michael G. Wilson of EON Productions for allowing me to reproduce the James Bond images on pp. 21–25 and 151–155. The James Bond films are (C) 1962–2015 Danjaq LLC and United Artists Corp, All Rights Reserved.

LucasFilm for kindly agreeing I could use images from my personal albums of *Star Wars: The Empire Strikes Back*. The Star Wars films are © & ™ Lucasfilm Ltd. All rights reserved.

Massimo Moretti of StudioCanal UK for supplying images from *The Rebel* and *Summer Holiday*.

Dave Worrall and Lee Pfeiffer of www.cinemaretro.com, for help with sourcing and researching photographs.

Andy Boyle, for his expertise in 'touching up' some of my old scratched, folded and dog-eared snaps.

Bob and Paul from Elstree Screen Heritage, for assisting with photos.

And last, but by no means least, my wife Titti who so often lost me to my 'den' (office) on many occasions, and for the patience and guidance she offered all along the way.

If you enjoyed this book, you may also be interested in …

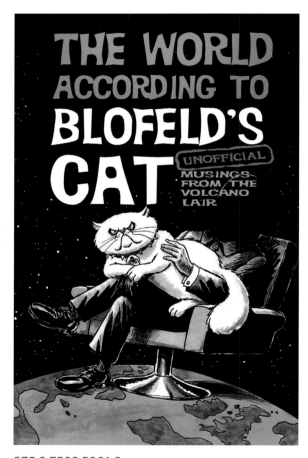

978 0 7509 5961 2

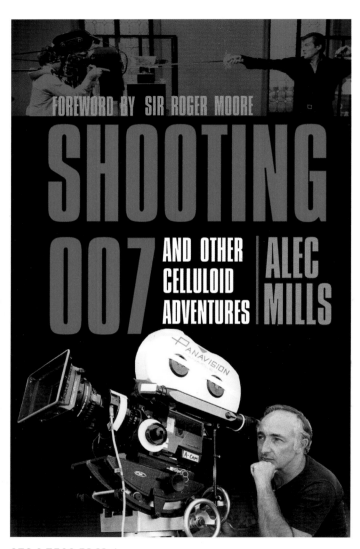

978 0 7509 5363 4